Snapshots of the Old Testament A Concise Summary of Every Book in the Old Testament

Lee J. Smith

March 2025

Snapshots of the Old Testament A Concise Summary of Every Book in the Old Testament Copyrights ©2025 by Lee J. Smith

eBook ISBN: 979-8-9929284-2-6

Paperback ISBN: 979-8-9929284-0-2

Hardcover ISBN: 979-8-9929284-1-9

Copyright Registration Number: TXu 2-479-581

All Scripture quotations are from the English Standard Version, (Crossway 2001)

Table of Contents

Introduction

My purpose in writing this little survey is to give students of the Bible a resource for understanding the historical context, basic argument and practical value of each book of the Old Testament of the Bible. I want the reader to have assurance that each book in the Bible has significance for understanding God's eternal plan and has value for personal spiritual development. I am totally convinced that 2 Timothy 3:16-17 speaks the truth: "All Scripture is breathed out by God and profitable for teaching, for reproof, for correction, and for training in righteousness, that the person of God may be complete, equipped for every good work."

This will not be a detailed study or a commentary. I do not intend to enter into academic debates about authorship, dates of composition, or the historical development of the books. Neither do I intend to prove the conclusions to which I have come.

This is intended to be a quick guide for non-theologically trained people who just want a better understanding of the basic content and practical application of each of the books of the Bible.

I write from an evangelical perspective, believing that the

books of the Bible are God's inspired, inerrant word, which gives us all we need to know to know God, gain eternal life, grow in Christlikeness, and do his will.

Some of the outlines are not original to me. Some are developed from professors at Dallas Theological Seminary. I noted the sources when I adopted an outline.

Neither you nor I will agree with everything in the recommended resources listed. I have placed an asterisk before the commentaries, which I would consider first buys.

A SNAPSHOT OF THE OLD TESTAMENT

Author: God the Holy Spirit is the author of the books of the Old Testament.

God superintended the human authors, using their experiences, vocabulary, and styles of writing, to write what God wanted to be written. [2 Peter 1:21]

Date of Events: The Old Testament story covers the entirety of human history from creation to the eternal future.

Date of Writing: The Old Testament was written over a span of 1000 years from about 1400 B.C. to about 400 B.C.

Original Languages: The original manuscripts of the Old Testament were written in Hebrew, except for parts of Daniel and Ezra, which were written in Aramaic.

Literary Forms of the Old Testament: The Old Testament contains many different literary forms, including narrative, poetry, prose, legal instruction, proverbs, songs, sermons, and prophecy.

Theme: The basic theme of the Old Testament is the Kingdom of God, the rule of God over the universe [Psalm 33:1-17] and over his people.

Purpose: The purpose of the Old Testament is to reveal who

God is and unveil his eternal plan to establish his eternal kingdom and deliver humankind from the consequences of sin through his Messianic King. This purpose includes displaying his glory and encouraging faith and obedience on the part of people.

The Story

The first eleven chapters of Genesis are the introduction to the Bible.

Four main events are recorded: (1) Creation--How we got here,(2) The Fall into Sin-- How we got into the mess we are in(3) The Flood--The event leading to the institution of human government and (4) Babel--How people were scattered over the world in differing cultures

In Genesis 12, God called Abram out of Ur and made a covenant with him. In this covenant, God promised him three things: A land to live in (Canaan), descendants (The Jewish People), and a blessing (which extends to all people). Abraham had two sons, Ishmael and Isaac. God chose Isaac. Isaac had two sons, Esau and Jacob. God chose Jacob. Jacob had twelve sons. The most important of these sons were Judah and Joseph. Judah was chosen to carry on the line of the Messiah. Joseph was used by God to save the lives of his brothers. Joseph was taken to Egypt as a slave. The whole

4

family followed him there and became a people. [Genesis]

Four hundred years later, in 1440 B.C., God brought the people out of bondage in Egypt under the leadership of Moses and Aaron by parting the waters of the Red Sea. God led them to Mt. Sinai, where he gave them the Law. This was a conditional covenant. It consisted of 613 commandments, which promised blessing if they obeyed the Law and cursing if they disobeyed. The Law governed their moral life (The Commandments), their social life (Judgments), and their worship (Ordinances). It specified the place of worship, the Tabernacle, the means of worship, the sacrifices, and special occasions for worship, the feasts. The history of Israel from this point on depended on their response to the Law. [Exodus/Leviticus/Deuteronomy]

At Kadesh-Barnea, they sent out spies to spy on the promised land of Canaan. Ten of the spies gave a bad report on the land. The people wanted to go back to Egypt. Two of the spies urged the people to trust God and proceed to Canaan. These two spies were Joshua and Caleb. Because of their unbelief, that generation was banished to wander in the wilderness for 40 years and die there. [Numbers]

After Moses died, Joshua became the leader. He led them across the Jordan River to conquer Canaan and divide the land into tribal areas. All the tribes received allotments except the tribe of Levi, which consisted of priests and religious leaders. [Joshua]

The next period of Israel's history after the death of Joshua was the time of the Judges. It was a period of ups and downs which became increasingly evil. The pattern of the times was of sin, slavery, supplication, and salvation: A pattern repeated over and over. Some of the Saviors God raised up in this period were Deborah, who defeated the Canaanites; Gideon, who defeated the Midianites; and Samson, who decimated the Philistines. The last judge was Samuel.

The evilness of these times demonstrated that the nation needed new leadership. So, God raised up a new type of spiritual leadership, the prophets, and a new type of political leadership, the kings. Samuel anointed the first two kings. The first king of the United Monarchy of Israel was Saul. He proved to be unfaithful and was set aside. God then chose David and gave him an unconditional covenant. In this covenant, found in 2 Samuel 7, God promised David an eternal kingdom which would be ruled by one of David's descendants forever. David wrote many of the Psalms. [1&2 Samuel/Psalms]

David was followed to the throne by his son, Solomon. This

wise man wrote many of the Proverbs as well as Ecclesiastes and The Song of Solomon. He also built the temple. After Solomon, the United Kingdom split into two kingdoms. The ten northern tribes broke away to form the kingdom of Israel. All the kings of Israel were wicked and followed false gods, so in 722 B.C. God allowed the nation of Assyria to destroy the nation and take many people away into captivity.

The descendants of David ruled over the southern kingdom of Judah, which consisted of the tribes of Judah and Benjamin. Some of the kings of Judah followed the Lord, and some were wicked. Overall, conditions kept getting worse. Some of the best-known of the good kings were Jehoshaphat [873-848 B.C.], Joash [835-796 B.C.], Hezekiah, who was encouraged by Isaiah [715-686 B.C.],

and Josiah [640-609 B.C.].

In 586 B.C. Nebuchadnezzar, king of Babylon, destroyed the city of Jerusalem and the temple and took away many exiles from Babylon. It was this destruction Jeremiah mourned in the book of Lamentations. [1&2Kings/1&2Chronicles/Proverbs/Ecclesiastes/SongSolo mon/Lamentations]

Seventy years later, Cyrus, king of Media-Persia, allowed the Jews to return to their land in fulfillment of the prophecy of Jeremiah. The book of Ezra tells the story of the rebuilding of the temple. Nehemiah tells the story of rebuilding the walls of Jerusalem. Esther tells how God spared the Jewish exiles from destruction during the reign of the Persian king, Xerxes. [Ezra/Esther/Nehemiah]

Where do the Prophets fit in? The ministry of the prophets arose during the period of the Judges but became prominent during the united and divided kingdoms. Three of the prophets whose books are recorded in Scripture primarily ministered to the northern kingdom of Israel: Hosea, Amos and Jonah. Seven of the prophets primarily ministered to the southern kingdom of Judah: Isaiah, Jeremiah, Joel, Micah, Nahum, Habakkuk and Zephaniah.

Four of the prophets ministered during the time of the Babylonian exile: Obadiah, Jeremiah, Ezekiel and Daniel. Three of them ministered during and after the return to Judah: Haggai, Zechariah and Malachi. Isaiah is noted for his many prophecies of the coming Messiah. Jeremiah contains the prophecy of the New Covenant, an unconditional covenant, promising a future physical restoration of the Jews to their land and a promise of their spiritual restoration. Jonah and Nahum prophecied against Nineveh, capital of Assyria and Obadiah prophesied against

Edom.

There are 400 years between the writing of Malachi and the first events of the New Testament. The last prophecy of Malachi was of the coming of Elijah which Jesus said referred to John the Baptist.

Basic Teachings of the Old Testament

1. The Old Testament is primarily a revelation from and about God. The character and will of God are revealed in his words, his actions, and his names. He is Elohim, the Mighty One, the sovereign creator of the universe who rules over all.

His personal name is Yahweh. I who I am. The eternally existing one who acts on behalf of his people, the God of the Covenants.

2. The Old Testament also reveals basic truth about people. We were created in the image of God to manage this world. [Genesis 1:26-28]. We are personal beings who think, feel, and make decisions. We are spiritual beings able to have a relationship with God and survive death. We are also fallen. [Genesis 3] We sin [Psalm 14:1-3] and are now sinners by nature [Psalm 51:5]. Sin leads to death and judgment. [Genesis 3]

3. The theological center of the Old Testament is the

Kingdom: the rule of God over the people of God.

a. God rules over the universe [Ps. 33:1-17]. Genesis 1-11 shows how mankind rejected the rule of God. God then elected to center his rule in a particular people, the people of Israel.

Genesis 12 through the end of the Old Testament centers on God's rule over his chosen people, the chosen line from Abraham, Isaac and Jacob.

God administers his rule through numerous agents primarily his word (Is. 40:8) and his Spirit (Gen. 6:3)

From Abraham to Sinai God ruled through the Patriarchs. From Sinai to the Judges he ruled through Moses, Joshua and the priests. In judges his rule was administered through the judges and the priests. From Samuel to the Exile it was administered through the kings, priests and prophets. From the Exile to Christ God ruled through the Gentile nations, the prophets, and the Remnant

b. The relationship between God and his people is regulated by covenants.

There are three unconditional covenants. The Abrahamic Covenant [Gen. 12:15], The Davidic Covenant [2 Sam 7], and The New Covenant [Jer. 31]. In these God promised to do certain things for his people. There are no conditions. There is one conditional covenant. This is the Law of Moses. After Sinai the life of the people was regulated by the Law of 613 regulations. Several ideas are central in the covenants: (1) Fellowship. By the sacrifices the OT believer demonstrated his faith and restored his fellowship with God. (2) Promise. Under the law obedience brought blessing and disobedience brought cursing (Deut. 28). The promises of the unconditional covenants are dependent only upon God's loyal love (hesed) and faithfulness (emet) (Mal. 1:2, Ps. 89:33).

(3) God's presence among his people.

Things which oppose the rule of God include: Satan (Gen 3), sin, death (Ps. 51), false religion (Paganism--worshipping false gods (1 Kings 16:31), and empty ceremonialism-- rituals without sincerity (Jer. 7:22).

The culmination of the rule of God is found in the prophesied reign of Messiah, a descendent of David who will usher in God's kingdom and provide forgiveness of sin. This we know is Jesus Christ, the Son of Abraham, Son of David and Son of God.

The Perimeters of the Old Testament

There are 39 books in the English Old Testament. These books were accepted as Scripture because the people of God recognized that these books contain within their pages the authoritative stamp of God's inspiration. The Traditional Hebrew Bible (containing the same books as our English Bible) was the Bible accepted by our Lord Jesus Christ and the early church. [Luke 11:51, 24:44] Neither the Jews, Christ, nor the early church accepted the Apocrypha as Scripture.

The Hebrew Bible was divided into three parts: (1) The Torah [Law] Genesis through Deuteronomy [The Pentateuch], (2) The Prophets including The Former Prophets [Joshua, Judges, 1&2 Samuel, 1&2 Kings] and The Latter Prophets [Isaiah, Jeremiah, Ezekiel, and Hosea through Malachi], and (3)The Writings including Wisdom and Poetry [Psalms, Proverbs, and Job], the Megilloth or "Rolls [The Song of Solomon, Ruth, Lamentations, Ecclesiastes, and Esther] and History [Daniel, Ezra/Nehemiah, and 1 & 2 Chronicles].

Applicational Value of the Old Testament

Applying the Old Testament to our lives in a proper way is not as easy as in the New Testament. An application is a change in a person's behavior (what he thinks, says, feels, or does) resulting from understanding the divinely-intended relationship between a biblical text and himself. Here are some guidelines:

1. Application is personal.

It may be pointed out by others, but it must be applied to life by the individual himself. A valid application must be perceived as valid and put into practice to have transforming value.

2. Valid applications are limited to the intention of the passage. Application is limited by:

a. The audience to whom the text was originally addressed and

b. The purpose of the author (divine and human).

3. Since the original audience of the Old Testament was not New Testament believers, we must be very careful in drawing direct applications from the Old Testament.

3. In applying the Old Testament distinctions between **direct applications** and universal principles must be carefully made. Direct applications apply to a specific group of people during a particular time period. **Universal principles** are

truths which are universally applicable and eternally valid. While the Old Testament contains a multitude of universal principles, the majority of "direct applications" for us as Church Age believers will come from texts which are directly addressed to us.

These cautions are not intended to downplay the spiritual value of the Old Testament. The New Testament makes it clear that the Old Testament is divine revelation which leads us to Christ and Christian maturity. When the New Testament authors speak of the Scriptures they are primarily speaking about the Old Testament. [Luke 24:27, 44-45, John 5:46, Romans 15:4, 1 Corinthians 10:1-11, 2 Timothy 3:16-17].

Recommended Resources

Gleason Archer, A Survey of Old Testament Introduction, Moody, 1964

Barry Beitzel, The Moody Atlas of Bible Lands, Moody, 1985

John Walvoord and Roy Zook, The Bible Knowledge Commentary: Old Testament, Victor, 2002

Roland de Vaux, Ancient Israel [2 volumes], McGraw-Hill, 1961

R.K. Harrison, <u>Old Testament Times</u>, Eerdmans, 1970

Walter Kaiser, <u>A History of Israel</u>, B & H, 1998

Tremper Longman III, <u>Making Sense of the Old Testament</u>, Baker, 1998

Victor Matthews and D. Benjamin, <u>Social World of Ancient Israel</u>, Hendrickson, 1993

*Christopher J. H. Wright, <u>The Mission of God</u>, IVP, 2006

A Snapshot of Genesis

Author

Moses. Jesus said that Moses wrote the Pentateuch. [Matthew 8:4; 19:7 Mark 7:10 Luke 16:26, 31; 24:24,44, John 7:19]. The other authors of Scripture concur in this. [Romans 10:5; 2 Chronicles 25:4]. This does not mean that Deuteronomy 34 could not have been written by another person, such as Joshua. Liberal theology denies it and teaches what is called the Documentary Theory of at least four divergent sources. [J, E, D, P]

Date of Events

From the creation of the world [10,000 to 15,000 B.C.] through the death of Joseph @ 1777 B.C.

Date of Writing

Before 1400 B.C. when Moses died in the plains of Moab, east of the Jordan River. [Deuteronomy 34] Were these writings of Moses collected and put together by one editor? Perhaps.

Recipients

The people of Israel as they conquered and settled down in the promised land. Joshua had the book of the Law. Joshua

Theme

The Sovereign God begins to choose out a people for himself.

Purpose: To show how God sovereignly called out a people for Himself despite the sinful failures of mankind. [The outworking of Gods plans]

Outline

1. Early History of the Human Race (1-11)

    1) Creation. Chapter 1-2

    2) The Fall into Sin 3

    3) The Flood 4-9

    4) The Spread of the Nations 10-11

2. Early History of the Chosen Race 12-50

    1) Abraham 12:1-25:18

    2) Isaac 25:19-26:35

    3) Jacob 27:1-36:43

    4) Joseph 37:1-50:26

Textual Outline (based on the phrase "This is the account of' or the book of the generations of")

1. Introduction 1:1-2:3
2. The record of the heavens and earth. 2:4-4:26
3. The record of the descendants of Adam 5:1-6:8
4. The record of the descendants of Noah **6:9-9:2**
5. The record of the descendants of the sons of Noah 10:1-11:9
6. The record of the descendants of Shem 11:10-26
7. The record of the descendants of Terah 11:27-25:11
8. The record of the descendants of Ishmael 25:12-18
9. The record of the descendants of Isaac 25:19-35:29
10. The record of the descendants of Esau 36:1- 37:1
11. The record of the descendants of Jacob. 37:2-50:26

The Story

Genesis gives us the early history of humanity from the creation of the universe to the spread of the nations after the incident at Babel. [Genesis 1-11]. It then gives us the early history of the chosen people of God, the Jews. This begins with the call of Abram out of Ur and the covenant God gave him. It takes us through the lives of Isaac, Jacob, and Joseph and finishes with the relocation of the sons of Jacob in the land of Egypt and the death of Joseph.

Characteristics and Points of Interest

1. Chapters 1-11 are in summary form. They are universal in

scope and focus on 4 events: Creation, the Fall, the Flood and Babel.

2. Chapters 1-11 are doctrinally foundational to the entire Bible. Here we learn the basics of who God is and who we are. We learn about sin, suffering, death, judgment and grace.

3. There are no valid reasons for rejecting the historicity of Genesis 1-11. This includes creation in six twenty-four-hour days and a universal flood.

Reasons for accepting creation in six twenty-four-hour days include: (1) The use of the terminology evening and morning, (2) The fact that the word for day (yom) when used with numbers is elsewhere in Scripture literal days.

4. Genesis is a book of beginnings: of creation, of human history, of sin, of conscience, of human government, of divine covenant making, of the people of Israel. The word "Genesis" means "beginnings."

5. Genesis 12-50 is detailed and limited in scope. It focuses on four key people: Abraham, Isaac, Jacob, and Joseph. Their lives are traced and can be chronologically divided by the various places they lived. (Abraham: Ur (11: 28), Haran (11:31), Shechem (12:4-7), Bethel (12:8-9), Beersheba

(21:1- 22:24) and Hebron (23:1).

6. The key to the development of Genesis is the phrase, "This is the account of" (NIV). Other translations use the words "the generations of or "the genealogical records of." [2:4, 5: 1, 6:9, 10:1, 11:10, 11:27, 25:1, 23:19, 36:1, 37:2]

7. The key theme of the book is God's sovereign actions in spite of human failure.

8. The building of altars and sacrifice to God is repeatedly mentioned. (Noah 8:20) (Abraham 13:18; 22:9) (Isaac 26:25) (Jacob 28:18, 31:54, 33:2, 35:7, 46:1)

9. The genealogical records of the sons of Noah are important for identifying the peoples who would surround the people of Israel and occupy Canaan.

10. The recording of the Covenant given to Abraham in Genesis 12 and the repetition of these covenant promises are very important to understanding the theology of the Old Testament. (Abraham 12-15, 22) (Isaac 26:51-5, 24 (Jacob 27:27-29, 28:4, 13, 14, 35:10-12)

11. The purpose of chapters 34 & 38 is to show why the family of Jacob needed to immigrate to the land of Egypt. (cf. 46:3, 34) In Canaan there was an acute danger that the family of Jacob would be assimilated into the Canaanite

people, culture and religion and lose their identity. In Egypt this would not happen for cultural reasons (46:3,34)

12. Jacob's spiritual journey progresses by means of four divine revelations: 28: 10-22, 32:1, 32:22-30 and 46:1-4.

Major Applications

1. Genesis teaches us major doctrinal truth about God, man, sin, death, judgment, grace, redemption, faith, and God's promises. For example, the account of the fall in Genesis 3 shows the basics of temptation but also the destructive consequences of sin. In Genesis God is shown to be both sovereign and holy but also gracious. We are shown to be both created in God's image and fallen.

2. Genesis gives us great assurance in that we have a sovereign God who is working out His purposes. (Abram, Genesis 12:1-3, 12:17, 20:6, 22:13, 24:1), (Isaac, 25:11; 26:12, 24) (Jacob 28:13-15, 35:5) (Joseph 45:4-8, 50:19-21, 39:2, 24, 42:28, 44:16)

3. Genesis teaches valuable lessons about the walk of faith. (Abraham Genesis 15:6, 12:4,7 8, 13:4, chapters 18 and 22) (Isaac 25:21, 26:25 (Jacob 28:13-15, 31:5-9, 32:2, 33:20, 35:7).

4. Genesis helps us see that God carries out his plan through fallible men who at times fail. Abraham 12:10-20, 16:1-3,

Isaac 25:28, 26:1-17, Jacob 27:1-33, 28:20-21, 29:30, 32:20, 37:3

5. Joseph is a tremendous example of a man who lived by obedience and faith. 39:7-9, 40:8, 41:14-16, 50:24-25.

Recommended Resources

John J. Davis, Paradise to Prison Baker Book House, 1971

Victor Hamilton, The Book of Genesis Chapters 1-17 and Genesis 18-50[NICOT] Eerdmans, 1990

Kenneth Matthews, Genesis, 2 Vols. Holman, 1996, 2005

*Allen P. Ross, Creation & Blessing. Baker, 1988

Bruce K. Waltke, Genesis, A Commentary. Zondervan, 2001

Edward J Young, Studies in Genesis One. Presbyterian and Reformed, 1999

A Snapshot of Exodus

Author

Moses

Date of writing

About 1400 B.C.

Date of events

From about 1570 B.C. (Exodus 1:8) to about 1439 B.C. (Exodus 40: 17) Most of the events occur within a period of a little more than one year.

Theme

The chosen people become God's Covenant Nation. God's power to free.

Purpose

To show how God redeemed His people from bondage and established them as His Covenant Nation. To show how God was fulfilling His promises to Abraham to make his seed into a great nation. To set forth redemption as the central point of Israel's faith — the reference point they looked back to for assurance (Exodus 20:2; 1 Kings 8:16.21; Psalms 105:26-38; Psalms 106:6-12; Acts 7:34-36).

Outline

1. The redemption of the people from bondage. 1-18

  1) Their subjugation in Egypt. 1-10

      (1) The oppression 1

      (2) The deliverer 2-4

      (3) Struggle with Pharaoh 5-10 (the plagues)

  2) Their Redemption 11:1-12:3

  3) Their migration to Sinai 12:37-18:27

2. The constitution of the Nation 19-40

  1) The introduction 19

  2) The commandments 20

  3) The judgments 21-24:11

  4) The ordinances 24:12-40:38

[The law was a treaty, a conditional covenant. It was their constitution.]

Characteristics and points of interest

1. Geographical movement from Goshen in Egypt to Mt. Sinai (a distance of about 100 miles).

2. Exodus is very important in that it shows:

  1) That God is fulfilling His promises to Abraham.

    (1) To make a great nation of his seed. Genesis 12:2,

      Exodus 12:40, 41

    (2) To bring them out of Egypt. Genesis 15:13-14,

      Exodus 1:7

  2) The central point of Israel's faith-redemption from

    bondage.

3. Why did the children of Israel need to go to Egypt?

  1) God had given the family of Abraham a unique position, a unique purpose, (Genesis 12:3) and a unique identity (Genesis 12:2). Jacob's sons had lost their sense of uniqueness and were in danger of intermingling (in their culture, religion, and marriage). Examples of this are seen in the actions of Dinah, Simeon and Levi (Genesis 34), Reuben (Genesis 35:22), and Judah (Genesis 38). In Egypt they were segregated and grew to be a distinct people. Unlike the Canaanites, the Egyptians wanted no social or marital relations with the Hebrews (Genesis 43:32; 46:31-34).

  2) For physical survival (Genesis 45:5-8, 50:20). In the

430 years they were in Egypt, they grew from a family of 70 (Exodus 1:5) (75, including Joseph and his two sons and Jacob and Leah (Acts 7:14) to 600,000 men (Exodus 12:37), a probable total around two million people.

4. In Exodus this people began on a journey to become a nation (theocracy). Nationhood involved 3 things: (1) a people, (2) a constitution, and (3) a land.

5. The Law of Moses is basically a covenant regulating the relationship between the Lord and His people.

1) It was made between Israel and God. (It was not made for us, but there are abiding moral principles and applicational truths.)

2) The purpose of the Law.

(1) It was a covenant between Israel and the Lord - governing their relationship with Him and each other (Exodus 19:5-6).

(2) It did not save them. Salvation was never a matter of keeping the law, but always a matter of faith (Acts 13:39; Galatians 2: 16; 3:21; Genesis 15:6)

(3) It was a rule of life for Israel, God's redeemed Old Testament people.

(4) In a broader sense, it revealed the depth of sin and the need for a Savior.

3) Relationship of the Law of Moses to the Church-age believer.

(1) The Law was a covenant between God and Israel.

(2) Christ fulfilled the Law (Matthew 5:17; Romans 10:4; 2 Corinthians 3; Galatians 3:24) 13

(3) The believer is not under the Law of Moses (Galatians 3:1-ff; 5:1). There are abiding moral principles behind the law which are eternally valid. The Ten Commandments summarize the moral law. All of these 10 are repeated in the New Testament, except for the Sabbath law.

6. The plagues were both a demonstration of the power of God and a judgment upon the idolatrous religious system of Egypt (Exodus 12:12). They also increased the faith of Israel (Exodus 6:6-8), and established the authority of Moses as God's leader (Exodus 4:4-5)

7. The Tabernacle in which atonement was made was precisely made according to divine instruction.

The Tabernacle

Article	Message To Israel	Typology
Brazen Altar	Atonement and Worship	Worship (Heb 13:15, Rom 12:1)
Laver	Cleansing	Cleansing (1 Jn 1:9, 1 Tm 2:21, Titus 3:5, Eph 5:25-26, Jn 13:10
Golden Altar of Incense	Prayer	Prayer (Heb 7:25, 13:15, 1 Jn 2:1)
Lamp Stand	Truth, direction	Truth, direction (2 Cor 4:4-6, Jn 8:12, Ps 119:11)
Bread Table	Provision	Provision (Jn 6:35, Phil 4:19)
The Ark	Atonement Presence of God	Salvation Gal 3:13, Rom 3:24-25, 5:2, Heb 13:10, Eph 1:8

8. The ordinances provided

1) A way for God to manifest His presence among His people (Exodus 25:8).

2) A way for God to reveal His glory (Exodus 40:34, 35).

3) A way for a sinful people to worship a holy God.

4) A picture of redemption in Christ.

9. Institution of the Passover Feast (Exodus 12) and offering of the first-born to God (Exodus 13).

The Story

The story begins with the people of Israel enslaved in Egypt. Hearing their cries God raised up Moses and Aaron to lead them out of Egypt. Pharaoh's refusal to let them leave brought on the ten plagues and the institution of Passover. God parted the water of the Red Sea to facilitate their escape. God provided for them in the wilderness and brought them to Mt Sinai where he gave them his Law which served as their constitution as was a conditional covenant. The book ends with the completion of the Tabernacle and the beginning of their worship rituals.

Major applications

1. The power of God to redeem and create a people for

Himself. This gives us confidence (Philippians 1:6; 4:19; Ephesians 1:19, 20).

2. The power of God over all other spiritual forces.

3. The faithfulness of God in keeping His promises.

4. The perversity of sin in our hearts. How soon the grumblings and unbelief set in!

5. The recognition of God's authority over every sphere of our lives is seen in that the law's regulations cover moral, civil, social, and religious areas.

   Note: These laws were beneficial laws which led to the welfare of the people.

 6. The authority of God over how He is to be worshipped is seen in the minute instructions for the Tabernacle. His worship is to be orderly and first class.

Recommended Resources

U. Cassuto, A Commentary on the Book of Exodus, Magnes, 1967

*John J. Davis, Moses and the Gods of Egypt, Baker, 1971

Duane Garrett, A Commentary on Exodus, Kregel, 2013

Gene Getz, Moses: Moments of Glory: Feet of Clay Regal Books, 1976

Victor Hamilton, Exodus: An Exegetical Commentary, Baker, 2011

Douglass Stuart, Exodus: An Exegetical and Theological Exposition, Holman , 2006

The Plagues

Scripture	Plague	False god
1. Ex. 7:14-25	Nile/blood	Osiris
2. Ex. 8:1-15	Frogs	Hekt
3. Ex. 8:16-19	Dust/lice	Seb
4. Ex. 8:20-32	Flies	Scarabaeus
5. Ex. 9:1-7	Murrain disease	Apis
6. Ex. 9:8-21	Dust/boils	Typlon
7. Ex. 9:22-35	Hail	Shu
8. Ex. 10:1-20	Locusts	Serapia
9. Ex. 10:21-29	Darkness	Ra
10. Ex. 11:1-12:30	Death	All gods

THE FEASTS OF ISRAEL

NAME	DATE	MEANING	TYPOLOGY
Passover Leviticus 23:5 Numbers 28:16-25	1st month 14th day	National life Redemption from bondage	Redemption 1 Peter 1:19
Unleavened bread Leviticus 23:6-8	1st month 15th-21st day	Holiness of Israel Separated people	Holy life 1 Corinthians 5:7-8
First fruits Leviticus 23:9-14	1st month 16th day	Thanksgiving Dedication	Resurrection of Christ 1 Corinthians 15:20
Pentecost (Weeks) Leviticus 23:15-21	3rd month 6th day	Consecration	Formation of the church Acts 2
Trumpets Leviticus 23:23-25	7th month 1st day	New year Calling together	Regathering of Israel Matthew 24:31
Atonement Leviticus 16; 23:26-32	7th month 10th day	Removal of sins	Conversion of Israel Zechariah 13:1
Tabernacles (Booths) Leviticus 23:33-ff	7th month 15th-22nd day	Thanksgiving/joy God's faithfulness in wilderness	Millennial joy Zechariah 14:16-21

33

A Snapshot of Leviticus

Author

Moses

Date of writing

Between Mt. Sinai and Moses' death (1438-1400 B.C.)

Date of events

At Mt. Sinai (1439-38 B.C.). There are only 3 historical events recorded in Leviticus: (1) The consecration of the priests (8 & 9), (2) The death of Nadab and Abihu (10) and (3) The stoning of the blasphemer (24:10-23).

A comparison of Exodus 40:17 with Numbers 1:1 shows that these events took place within a month.

Theme

Living a holy life before a holy God.

Purpose

To give the priests a handbook of regulations for the worship of Israel.

To reveal how the people of God could live a holy life in the presence of a holy God.

Outline

1. The worship of a holy God (1-16).

  1) By sacrifice (1-7)

    (1) Burnt (1)

    (2) Meal (2) .

    (3) Peace (3)

    (4) Sin (4:1-5:13)

    (5) Trespass (5:14-6:7)

      Note: 6:7-7:38 are special instructions pertaining to each

        offering.

  2) By the ministry of the priests (8-10)

    (1) Consecration of Aaron and sons (8)

    (2) Inauguration of the sacrificial system (9)

    (3)Transgression of the sacrificial system by Nadab and
Abihu (10)

  3) By ceremonial purification (11-15)

    (1) Food laws (11)

    (2) Laws about childbirth (12)

(3) Laws about leprosy (13-14)

(4) Laws about bodily discharges (15)

4) By the Day of Atonement (16)

2. The walk before a holy God 17-27

1) The holiness of the people (17-20)

(1) In relationship to the sacrifices (17)

(2) In relationship to marriage (18)

(3) In relationship to God's law (19-20)

2) The holiness of the priests (21-22)

3) The holiness of special things and occasions

(1) The Sabbath (23:3-8)

(2) The feasts (23:9-44)

(3) Other sacred holy things and occasions (24-25)

4) Blessings and cursings (26)

5) Holiness of vows (27)

The Story

Leviticus does not advance the story very much. At the time of Leviticus the Israelites were at Mt. Sinai. Only three incidents are mentioned.

Characteristics and points of interest:

1. Leviticus contains more of the direct words of God than any other Old Testament book.

2. That holiness is the theme is seen in the use of the Hebrew root for holy (kadosh) 110 times: noun 79 times, verb 31 times.

3. Leviticus serves as a worship handbook for the priests.

4. There is a progression in regulations dealing in order with:

   1) The place of worship (Exodus 35-40)

   2) Rituals (sacrifices) (Leviticus 1-7)

   3) Clergy/priests) (8-10) and various situations (11-27)

5. Requirements imposed upon the priests were higher than for a common person (21-22)

6. The phrase "I am the Lord" is repeated 50 times. Worship should arise out of and lead to a recognition of the holiness of God.

7. Leviticus is a part of the Covenant Law which began in Exodus 20. Like all covenants of that time, it concludes with a statement of blessings for obedience and cursings for disobedience. (26).

8. The clean unclean and holy vs. common terminology is

important in the theology of Leviticus.

9. The purpose of the sacrifices was to allow sinful people to worship and fellowship with the holy God. They were to Israelite believers what 1 John 1:9 is to us.

Major applications

1. Be holy for I am holy. 1 Peter 1:13-16; 2 Corinthians 6:14-7:1

2. The grace of God in providing a means by which the believer can come into the presence of God and have fellowship.

3. The need of cleansing before service (Leviticus 8). High standards God expects in spiritual leaders.

4. The sinfulness of sin. Sin separates us from a holy God.

5. The omniscience of God - as seen in the typology.

6. Gratitude - No longer do we have a sacrificial system because of the sufficiency of Christ's death.

Recommended Resources

Andrew Bonar, Leviticus, Banner of Truth, 1966

John Hartley, Leviticus, Word, 1992

Andrew Jukes, The Law of the offerings, Kregel, 1976

*Alan P. Ross, Holiness to the Lord. Baker, 2002

G.J. Wenham, The Book of Leviticus, Eerdmans, 1979

Christopher J. H. Wright, Old Testament Ethics for the People of God, IVP, 2004

The Levitical Offerings

	Lev. 1:3-17; 6:8-13	Lev. 2:1-6; 6:14-18	Lev. 3:1-17; 7:11-38	Lev. 4:1-5:13; 6:24-30	Lev. 5:14-6:7; 7:1-7
	Burnt	**Grain**	**Fellowship**	**Sin**	**Guilt**
Nature of offering	1. Bull, sheep, goat or young pigeons. 2. Depended on economic status of offerer. 3. Male only.	1. Unbaked flour, unleavened cakes or roasted grain. 2. Olive oil, salt, incense added. 3. No leaven or honey, no fermentation or corruption.	1. Bull, lamb or goat. 2. Male or female.	1. Priest--bull 2. Congregation--bull 3. Ruler--male goat 4. Ordinary person -- female goat or lamb, 2 turtledoves or pigeons, 1/10 ephah flour.	1. Against God, 5:15-19 ram of required value. 2. Against man--ram of required value, 6:1-7.
Ritual for offerer	1. Bring to door of Tabernacle. 2. Put hand on head. 3. Kill, skin & cut in pieces. 4. Sheep or goat--kill on north side of the altar.	1. Prepare according to directions. 2. Bring to door of Tabernacle. 3. Give to priest.	1. Bring to door of Tabernacle. 2. Put hands on head. 3. Kill. 4. Give fat, caul (membrane above kidneys), kidneys to priest. 5. Offer with a grain offering.	1. Put hands on head (elders for congregation). 2. Kill.	1. Put hands on head. 2. Kill. 3. Pay restitution--full payment plus 20% for damages.
Ritual for priest	1. Sprinkle blood around bronze altar. 2. Lay parts in order on altar. 3. Wash and burn. 4. Remove ashes outside camp.	Burn a portion with oil and incense on altar.	1. Catch, sprinkle blood. 2. Burn caul, kidneys, fat tail of sheep. 3. Wave breast horizontally, heave thigh vertically.	1. Place blood on altars of incense or bronze, offering for ordinary person or ruler on bronze altar. 2. Burn fat or grain. 3. Burn remains of bull outside camp for priest or congregation	1. Sprinkle blood around altar. 2. Burn fat on altar.
God's portion (brazen altar)	All, except skin.	The portion burned on altar, representative of the whole.	Fat of the entrails (a delicacy preferred by Eastern people but required by God).	Fat of the entrails, 4:9-10.	Fat of the entrails, 7:3-7

	Lev. 1:3-17; 6:8-13	Lev. 2:1-6; 6:14-18	Lev. 3:1-17; 7:11-38	Lev. 4:1-5:13; 6:24-30	Lev. 5:14-6:7; 7:1-7
	Burnt	**Grain**	**Fellowship**	**Sin**	**Guilt**
Priest's portion	Skin of animal, 7:8	All that remained 2:3; 6:16-18	1. Wave breast for priestly family. 2. Heave thigh for officiating priest.	Portion of offering of ruler & laymen, 6:26, 30.	Portion not burned on altar, 7:6.
Offerer's portion			All that remained shared by family and friends in court of Tabernacle.		
Meaning to offerer	1. A voluntary act of worship. 2. Complete surrender to God of individual or congregation. 3. Recognition--way to God by sacrifice	1. A voluntary act of worship. 2. Recognition of God's goodness, provision of necessities of life. 3. Yielded life, now laancs of hands.	1. A voluntary act of worship. 2. Types--thanksgiving, 7:12; vow 7:16; voluntary offering, 7:16) 3. Recognition that fellowship with God restored on basis of sacrifice.	1. Obligatory offering. 2. Recognition that sin must be dealt with whether by priest, ruler, individual, etc. 3. Recognition that forgiveness of sin came through offering a substitutionary sacrifice.	1. Obligatory offering. 2. Recognition that sin causes injury to God and man. 3. Recognition that the sinner must offer a sacrifice as a substitute for himself and must make restitution or compensation for his sin.
Typology	1. Christ's vicarious death for redemption of sinners 2. Christ offering Himself to God in death, a complete yielding to the Father, cf. Heb. 9:14; 10:5-7; Eph. 5:2	1. Christ offered to God a perfect life which gave efficacy to His death. Rarely offered alone	1. Christ made peace by the cross Col. 1:20. 2. On the basis of His sacrifice we have fellowship with God. He is our peace offering.	1. Christ is our sin offering. He died that our sins might be forgiven (2 Cor. 5:21; Eph. 1:7). 2. Men must identify with Jesus Christ, the sin offering, in a personal way if they want forgiveness.	1. Christ in His death atoned for the damage, the injury of sin. (cf. Psalm 51:4) 2. In Isaiah 53:10 Messiah is designated as a trespass offering.

40

A Snapshot of Numbers

Author

Moses

Date of Writing

@1400 B.C.

Date of Events

@1438-1400 B.C.

Recipients

The Israelites

Theme

Israel Under God's Training in the Wilderness

Purpose

1. To show how God prepared His people physically and spiritually to enter the Promised land.

2. God's blessings of Israel cannot be frustrated despite Israel's failures.

3. To demonstrate the out-working of the principles of the Mosaic Covenant.

The Story

Numbers begins at Mt. Sinai. Chapters 1-10 are preparations for their departure from Mt. Sinai.

After the consecration of the Tabernacle and the celebration of Passover the Israelites left Mt. Sinai. The book records the numerous complaints of the people, the punishments God sent, and the provisions God provided in the wilderness. Spies were sent to spy out Canaan. The people refused to advance and threatened Moses. God condemned them to wandering in the wilderness until that generation died. Other events recorded include Korah's rebellion, water from the rock, the disobedience of Moses, the deaths of Miriam and Aaron, the bronze snake, the defeat of King Sihon and King Og, the story of Balaam, and the taking of a second census. The book ends in the plains of Moab east of the Jordan River.

Outline

1. Preparation to Depart from Sinai 1:1-10:10

   1) Numbering and arrangement 1-4

   2) Final instructions 5:1-10:10

2. From Sinai to the Plains of Moab 10: 11-21:35

   1) Sinai to Par an, travel troubles 10-12

2) The great rebellion 13-14

3) The wilderness wanderings 15-19

3. In the Plains of Moab 22-36 (preparation for entering the land)

1) The Balaam oracles 22-24

2) Sin with Midian 25

3) Renumbering 26-27

4) Various laws 28-30

5) Notable events 31-32

6) Historical summary 33

7) Final words 34-

Characteristics and Points of Interests

1. The two numberings of the people Chapters 1 & 2 and 26 shows the faithfulness of God in preserving His people.

2. The efforts made to show the preparation of Israel to enter the land. A new generation [26:63-65] , New leaders [34:16-29] (Miriam, Aaron, and Moses die; Eleazar and Joshua arise) [20:28, 27:18-23]

3. Further elaborations of the Law: Levitical duties (3-4), test

of adultery (5), Nazirite law (6), offerings (15,18 ,28, 29), purification rites (19), vows (30), cities of refuge (35), and inheritance regulations (36)

4. The Balaam oracles, 22-24, show that the purpose of God to bring Israel to the Promised Land could not be thwarted.

5. Numbers includes both historical & legal materials.

Major Applications

1. Teaching on the goodness and severity of God.

2. The importance of obedience of a single person. (Moses)

3. The warning of the consequences of sin and the blessings of obedience. cf. 1 Corinthians 10: 6-11

4. As an illustration of God's work in preparing His people for their inheritance.

5. To show that the purposes of God will not be thwarted by the sinfulness of people. (His own people or the ungodly)

6. The orderliness God desires we have in our lives is seen in Numbers.

Recommended Resources

Ronald B. Allen, Numbers (Expositor's Bible Commentary), Zondervan, 2017

Timothy Ashley, <u>The Book of Numbers</u> (NICOT), Eerdmans, 1993

Irving L. Jensen, <u>Numbers: Journey to God's Rest-Land</u>, Moody Press, 1964

*Gordon J. Wenham, <u>Numbers: An Introduction and Commentary</u>, IVP, 2008

A Snapshot of Deuteronomy

Author

Moses (essentially)

Date of Events

@ 1400 B.C.

Date of Writing

@ 1400 B.C.

Recipients

The new generation of Israelites about to enter the Promised Land

Theme

The faithful God demands obedience from His servants.

Purpose

To encourage faithful obedience to the Lord.

Outline

1. The Preamble 1:1-5

1) The name of the mediator Moses

2) The place of the agreement.

3) The historical situation

2. The Historical Prologue. 1:6-4:49

This is a historical review of how God, the great King, had benefited his people and how they had rebelled against him. This includes an initial appeal to obey what he is about to teach them. 4:1-14 and warnings about what will happen if they turn to idolatry. 4:15-31. Note: Passages about passing on the story 4:9-10, 6:5-7, 20-ff.

3. The Rules of the Covenant

  1) The great commandments. 5:1 11:32

    (1) The ten basic rules. 5:1-33

    (2) The command to love the Lord. 6:1-25

    (3) Commands concerning relationships to the nations.

      7:1-26

    (4) Warning not to forget the Lord. 8:1-20

    (5) Reminder of the future. 9:1-10:11

    (6) Command to fear the Lord. 10:12-22

    (7) Command to obey the Lord. 11:1-31

  2) The Secondary commands. 12:1-26:10

(l) Ceremonial rules. 12:1-16:

a. The place of worship. 12:1-32

b. Warmings against worshipping false gods. 13:1-18

c. Teaching about clean and unclean foods. 14:1-21

d. The Tithes 14:22-25

e. The Sabbatical year. 15:1-18 Note on v. 16

f. The Firstborn 15: 19-23

g. The Feasts. 16:1-17

(2) Social and civil regulations. 16:18 —21:23

a. Judges 16.18-20

b. Dealing with idol worshippers. 16:21-17:7

c. Legal cases. 17:8-13

d. Regulations for the king. 17:14-20

e. Offerings for the priests and Levites. 18:1-8

f. Forbidding pagan practices. 18:9-13

g. Rules about prophets. 18: 14-22

h. Cities of Refuge. 19:1-14

i. The necessity of legal witnesses. 19:15-21

j. Rules for war. 20:1-20

k. Atonement for unsolved murders. 21:1-9

l. Marriage to captives. 21:10-14

m. The Rights of firstborn. 21: 15-17

n. Dealing with rebellious children. 21: 18-21

o. Rules about bodies of executed people. 21: 22-23

(3) Social and Economic rules. 22:1-26:15

a. Various rules 22:1-12

b. Marriage rules. 22:13-30

c. Rules about exclusion. 23:1-8

d. Rules about toiletry. 23:9-14

e. More miscellaneous rules. 23:15-25:19

f. Firstfruits and tithes. 26:1-15

3. Summary 26:16-19

4. The Covenant Sanctions. 27:1-20:20

This section has to do with how the covenant is to be ratified when they enter Canaan.

1) The place and preparations. 27:1-8

2) The curses 27:9-26

3) The blessings 28:1-14

4) Further curses. 28:15-68

5) Call to affirm the covenant. 29:1-30:2

5. Disposition of the Covenant. Ch 31:1-34:12

  1) Arrangements for a new leader. 31:1-8

  2) Command to read the covenant. V.9-13

  3) Joshua is commissioned. 31:14-23

  4) Commands about storing the covenant v. 24-29

  5) The Song of Moses 31:30-32:52 Moses is a covenant witness.

  6) Moses' blessing of the people. 33:1-29. (He is 120 years old)

  7) The death of Moses and succession of Joshua. 34:1-12

The Story

Deuteronomy does not advance the story greatly. It begins and ends in the plains of Moab near the Jordan River. In a series of messages Moses rehearses the history of Israel from Mt. Sinai. He restates the law to this new generation. He issues a set of blessings and cursings. The book ends with a reading of the Law to the people, the commissioning of Joshua as Moses' successor, and the details of Moses' death.

Characteristics and Points of Interest

1. The Nature of the Book.

Essentially the book is a series of messages given by Moses, which have been brought together in the form of a covenant renewal document. Deuteronomy is the covenant document prepared by Moses to witness the renewal of the Sinai Covenant.

2. The Setting of the Book.

This is a new generation. The previous one had perished in the wilderness. Before they entered the land to conquer it, the covenant made by the Israelites with God at Sinai needed to be restated and reaffirmed by this new generation.

3. The Unique Structures of the Book.

Deuteronomy has the form of an ancient treaty kings forced on their subject peoples (vassals). It includes: a preamble in which the king was identified, a historical prologue outlining how the king had benefited the vassal and why he should gratefully obey him, regulations and stipulations which outlined the duties of the vassal toward the king, sanctions, provision for deposit of the document in the temple, instructions for periodic public reading and the invocation of witnesses.

Major Applications

1. God demands obedience from His servants. Obedience which should arise from gratitude for what he has done for his people. 4:35-40

2. The principle of blessings/cursings (28) Note: this is not the method of salvation.

3. The continued value of the Word of God-was to be kept and read and passed on. (6, 31:24-29)

4. The relevance of God's Word. Christ quoted Deuteronomy more than any other book.

5. Humble recognition of our position before the Sovereign Lord. (9:4-6; 7 6-8)

6. The importance of faithful good leadership. Joshua was trained by Moses. (34:9) Sometimes we lose something in our modern method of grooming church leaders. Joshua had spent 40 years with Moses. 2 Timothy 2:2

Recommended Resources

Paul A. Barker, <u>The Triumph of Grace in Deuteronomy</u>, Paternoster , 2004

Daniel I. Block, <u>The Gospel According to Moses</u> Cascade, 2012

George A. F. Knight, <u>The Song of Moses</u>, Eerdmans, 1995

*J. G. McConville, <u>Deuteronomy</u>, Apollos and IVP, 2002

Christopher J. H. Wright, <u>Deuteronomy</u>, Baker, 1994

A Snapshot of Joshua

Author

Unstated in the biblical text - probably primarily Joshua with additions after his death.

Date of Events

@ 1400 to @ 1380

In Joshua 14:10 Caleb says that it had been 45 years since God had promised him inheritance in the land of Canaan. He is referring to the promise recorded in Deuteronomy 1:36 and Numbewrs 14:30, 38. Numbers 14 took place during the second year after they had left Egypt (Num 10:11), If we accept 1440 B.C. as the date of the Exodus, then the date of Numbers 14 would be @ 1393.

The final events in Joshua take place an unspecified "long time afterward." (13:1) So, perhaps @ 1380 is a reasonable suggestion.

At this time Egypt was the world power which had control of Canaan.

Date of Composition

Within 25 years after Joshua's death. @1385-1380 B.C.

1. The author may have been an eyewitness and participant to many of the events. Some of the Hebrew manuscripts read "we" in 5: 1 ,6.

2. The phrase "to this day" 4:9, 5:9, 6:25, 7:26, 9:27. Rahab was still living. 6:25

3. The Jebusites still control Jerusalem 15:63

4. In Joshua Sidon is more prominent than Tyre which was not true in later history.

Theme

God's power and faithfulness in overcoming the enemies and in keeping his covenant promise of the land.

Purpose

To provide an official and authoritative account of God's faithfulness in leading his people to conquer the promised land. 21:43-45

Outline

1. Preparation for the Conquest 1:1-5:12

   1) Joshua commissioned 1:1-9

   2) The people prepared 1:10-2:24

   3) The crossing of the Jordan 3:5-5:1

Characteristics and Points of Interest

1. The history of the conquest is not developed chronologically but rather geographically.

2. God's edict of extermination against the Canaanites is not at all unjust when one: (1) understands the extent of their depravity. Joshua 11:20, Genesis 15: 15, Leviticus 18:24-25, (2) remembers that it is only by God's mercy that he chooses to spare anyone from judgment.

3. The "hornets" prophesied as going before Israel to drive out the enemies probably do not refer to insects but are either: (1) A symbol of fear. Exodus 23:27, Deuteronomy 7:20, Joshua 24: 12 "I will send over them fear and dread of you" or (2) The soldiers of Pharaoh Thutmose Ill who had established limited control of Palestine at the time. Thutmose had subjugated 100 petty kings in Palestine. His soldiers had the hornet as an emblem on their helmets.

4. The purpose of the miraculous crossing of the Jordan was: (1) to bolster their faith. 4:21-24 The new generation had not seen the opening of the Red Sea, (2) To create disabling fear in the hearts of the Canaanites (5: 1), (3) To assure the Israelites that God's purpose that they conquer the promised land had not changed, and (4) to confirm the authority of Joshua. 3:7, 4:14

5. The scattering of the Levitical Cities throughout the tribes

seems to be tied to the idea that they would permeate the land and have wide influence.

6. The central point of the book is to demonstrate that God faithfully kept his promise to give His people the promised land. This is emphasized in repeated statements about the completion of the task. [10:40-42, 21:43-45, 22:4, and 23:14

7. The seeds of future defeat: division and idolatry are seen in 9, 10:20, 13:2,13, 15:63, 16:10, 17:12-13, 18:32, 22:7-34, 23:7, 24:14, 23]

The Story

The story begins with God's command to Joshua to begin the conquest. The story leads from the Jewish espionage in Jericho, the crossing of the Jordan, the circumcision of the new generation to the first Passover in Canaan.

Chapters 5:13-2:24 detail the conquest from Jericho to the taking of northern Canaan. 12:25-2:24 tells of the division of the land into tribal areas, and the designation of cities of refuge and Levitical cities. The book ends with Joshua last words to the leaders, a covenant renewal at Shechem, and Joshua's death.

Major applications

Primarily, applications are to the life of the believer - how to find victory. There are many lessons about living in the land of fellowship and service.

1. The need for faithful obedience to the Word of God for victory in the Christian life

2. Dependence upon God's strength and wisdom is necessary in the spiritual struggle for victory. 9:14

3. The battle is not over. (13:2) There are still Canaanites to be beaten. The danger of compromise (23:13) with the pockets of sin in our lives. God is only satisfied with full obedience.

Note: In Joshua, we see that even amid victory are seeds of failure which lead to the downfall of Israel and Judah later. 13:2-4

4. Obedience comes from faith in the promises of God. Trusting God leads to obeying God.

5. God has a right to judge those who reject Him and His ways

6. Consecration precedes conquering. [5:2-12]

7. One who actively seeks God's control and willingly obeys God's Word will find spiritual success.

8. The traditional comparison of Canaan to heaven is not all

that helpful.

Recommended Resources

Donald K. Campbell and Jim Denney, No Time for Neutrality, Victor, 1994

John J. Davis, Conquest and Crisis, Baker Book House, 2008

Stanly Gundry, Show Them No Mercy: God and the Canaanites. Zondervan, 2003

Richard S. Hess, Joshua: An Introduction and Commentary, IVP, 2008

David M. Howard, Joshua: An Exegetical and Theological Exposition, Holman, 1998

*M.H. Woudstra, The Book of Joshua, (NICOT) Eerdmans, 1981

A Snapshot of Judges

Author

Unstated. Tradition points to Samuel

Date of Events

From the oppression of Babylon to the death of Samson. @300 to 330 years. [1380 B.C.-1050 B.C.] The period of the judges ends with Samuel in 1 Samuel 7. [The reference in 1 Kings 6:1 that it was 480 years from the Exodus to the beginning of the temple construction demonstrates that one cannot merely add up the years of oppression and judges to figure the time span of the period of the judges.]

Date of Composition

It was after the kingdom had begun (17:6, 18:1, 19:1, 21:25). It was before David drove the Jebusites out of Jerusalem (1:21 compared with 2 Samuel 5). @ 1010 B.C.

Recipients

Israel during the early United Monarchy.

Theme

Sin leads to death.

God's repeated faithfulness in spite of Israel's repeated

unfaithfulness (2:11-17)

Purpose

To show the failure of the theocracy under the priests and the necessity for God's new method of rule through kings and prophets.

Outline

1. The Failure of the Theocracy.**1:1-3:7**

   1) Failure in the past. 1:1-2:9

   2) Failure in the present. 2:10-3:6

2. The Deliverers of the Theocracy. 3:7-16:31

   1) In the south. 3: 7-31

      (1) Othniel 3:7-11

      (2) Ehud 3:12-30

      (3) Shamgar 3 1

   2) In the north. 4:1-5:31 Deborah and Barak.

   3) In the central region. 6:1-10:5

      (1) Gideon and Abimelech 6: 1-9:57

      (2) Tola 10:1-2

(3) Jair. 10:3-5

4) East of the Jordan River 10:6-12:15

   (1) Jephthah 10:6-1

   (2) Ibzan 12:8-10

   (3) Elon 12:11-12

   (4) Abdon 12:13-15

5) In the (Coastal) west: Samson

3. The Conditions in the Theocracy 17:1-21:25

   1) Religious Apostasy 17:1-18:31

     (1) Personal and Individual - Micah Judges 17

   2) Moral Decay 19:1-21:25 (1) Personal 19 (2) Tribal 20-21

The Story

Judges begins with a review of events which transpired after the death of Joshua, the conquests and failures in a summary way.

It progresses through a series of oppressions by various enemies and God's delivering the people through various military leaders who are called judges. Notable among these

63

are Othniel, Deborah and Barak, Gideon and Samson. This is not so much arranged chronologically as it is geographically. The book ends with examples of the moral and spiritual corruption of the people. The final verse reads, "In those days there was no king in Israel. Everyone did what was right in his own eyes," [Judges 21:25 ESV] setting the stage for the rise of prophets and kings.

Characteristics and Points of Interest

1. Judges is not developed strictly chronologically but geographically and thematically.

2. The historical setting Egypt is the dominant world power, the sea-peoples including the Philistines have invaded the coastal regions. The Israelites are mainly in the hills. The Canaanites control the valleys.

3. The Judges were raised up by God because of the failures of the priests. They were called by God to cast out the enemy and to uphold the covenant law of God. (2:18) They were not kings nor administrators but military saviors.

4. The ministries of some judges overlap one another.

5. The different oppressions may not have touched all twelve tribes.

6. The cycle of the book is set forth in 2:11-17 sin, slavery, supplication and salvation. (cf. also 3:5-9)

7. There is a downward spiral in Judges.

8. The period of the Judges does not end with the Book of Judges but continues through 1 Samuel

Major Applications

1. The danger of spiritual apostasy.

2. The mercy of God - His repeated sending of deliverers.

3. The danger of turning spiritual victory into spiritual defeat. Joshua 21:43-45

4. The danger of compromise. 1:19,21,27,28,29,30,31,32

5. The necessity of meeting God's tests. 2:20-23

6. The danger of wrong companions 3:5-7 Progress of sin.

7. The lack of moral self-restraint leads to the loss of personal freedom.

8. Spiritual apostasy will always lead to moral failure.

9. When spiritual leadership fails, God must raise up new leadership.

Recommended Resources

Robert Chisholm, A Commentary on Judges and Ruth, Kregel, 2013

John J. Davis, Conquest and Crisis Baker Book House, 2008

Gary Inrig, Hearts of Iron, Feet of Clay Moody, 1979

Barry G. Webb, <u>The Book of Judges</u> (NICOT), Eerdmans, 2012

*Leon Wood, <u>Distressing Days of the Judges</u>, Zondervan, 1975

A Snapshot of Ruth

Author

Unknown

Date of Events

[1:1] In the days of the Judges, perhaps at time of Gideon. Judges [6:3, 4]

Date of Writing

After David became king. 4:17, 22

Recipients

Israel during the monarchy.

Theme

God's providential care of those who walk with Him.

Purpose

1. To show God's sovereign providence in a degenerate time

2. To assure Israel that God is sovereign and at work even when He seems to be silent.

3. To show how God sovereignly, but in a hidden way, effected the birth of His chosen king, David.

4. To show the piety of the ancestors of King David, and God's Grace.

Outline

1. Discouragements 1

2. Discoveries 2

3. Decisions 3

4. Developments 4

The Story

A Jewish man, Elimelech, left Bethlehem with his wife Naomi and their sons and migrated to Moab because of a famine. The two sons married Moabite women, Orpah and Ruth. Elimelech and the two sons died. Naomi decided to return to Judah and encouraged her widowed daughters-in-law to stay in Moab. Ruth insisted on going with Naomi. In the process of gleaming grain for Naomi and her to eat, Ruth met Boaz a relative of Elimelech. Through a series of events Boaz agreed to marry Ruth and redeem Elimelech's property. Boaz and Ruth become the great grandparents of King David.

Characteristics and Points of Interest

1. Ruth and Boaz are the great grandparents of King David.

2. Gleaning - The poor, the widows, and the orphans had the right to follow the reapers and pick up what was left on the ground and in the corners of the field. Leviticus 19:9-10, 23:22, Deuteronomy 24:19-22]

3. Levirate Marriage [Genesis 38, Deuteronomy 25:5-10] What we see in Ruth is not strictly a Levirate marriage. Boaz was not a brother and not duty bound by the law to marry her. By the custom of the day, it was an honorable thing to do within the intended purpose of the Levirate Law. [4:10]

4. Redemption of the Land. A separate duty from the Levirate marriage. [Leviticus 25:8-ff]. All property was returned to the original family ownership on the Jubilee year. If property had to be sold (to sustain life) the nearest relative was to buy it back - to keep it in the family. The near relative or go'el (Kinsmen Redeemer) had other responsibilities as well.

1) To buy a relative out of slavery.

2) To avenge his murder.

Note: So, what was the man's issue in 4:1-6? If it had been the land redemption the man would have done it, but he did not want to take the Levirate duty because the money he had invested in Naomi's (Elimelech and sons) property would have been lost as the property would revert to the child born to Ruth as (legal heir of Mahlon) "No profit in it for himself."

5. The Shoe Removal Not the same as in (Deuteronomy 25:7-9). Here the shoe is a symbol of rights of possession. So, in handing the shoe to Boaz he is acknowledging that he is abrogating his rights as the near kinsmen and giving those rights over to Boaz.

Major Applications

1. The providence of God. God is active in the lives of His children. There are nine prayers to God for blessing upon others in the book - each of these requests is answered.

2. The Sovereignty of God. The chief actor in Ruth is God. He is in control in the midst of troubled times. Nothing happens apart from His permission and plan.

Note: The hiddenness of God. No one in Ruth hears the voice of God, sees a vision, or has a dream. There are no class "A" miracles. Nowhere does the author say - now see this is what God is doing. There are no prophets or priests. The people are acting freely of their own volition, following their own plans. Yet God is obviously in control of all that transpires.

3. God blesses those who remain loyal to Him, regardless of the problematic age in which they live. 2:12, 2:20, 3:9-10

4. Consequences of walking out of fellowship.

5. Boaz -type of Christ- our kinsman redeemer

6. Grace of God - Ruth a Moabite is included in the lineages of David and Jesus Christ.

Recommended Resources

Robert Alter, <u>Strong as Death is Love</u>, Norton, 2021

Cyril J. Barber, <u>Ruth</u> Moody Press, 1989

Daniel l. Block, <u>Judges and Ruth,: An Exegetical and Theological Exposition</u>, Holman, 1999

Robert Chisholm, <u>A Commentary on Judges and Ruth, Kregel</u>, 2013

Paul P. Enns, <u>Ruth</u> Zondervan, 1982

Murray D. Gow, <u>The Book of Ruth: Structure, Theme and Purpose,</u> Apollos, 1992

*Robert Hubbard, <u>The Book of Ruth</u>, (NICOT) Eerdmans, 1988

A Snapshot of 1st & 2nd Samuel

Author

Unknown

Date of Writing:

Unknown, probably after division of Kingdom which took place in 931 B.C.[1 Samuel 27:6]

Date of Events

Covers a period of around 80 years: 1 Samuel 1050 B.C. - 1010 B.C. [Saul, Samuel, David to death of Saul]; 2 Samuel 1010 B.C.- 970 B.C., the reign of David.

Recipients

The Jewish people after the division of The Kingdom.

Theme

God's king must obey Him.

Purpose

The purpose is not just to give biographies of Samuel, Saul and David, but to record the establishment of the visible Kingdom of God on earth in The Kingdom of Israel.

Outline

1. The End of the Judges 1 Samuel 1:1-7:17

2. The Reign of Saul 8-15

    1) His beginning 8-12

    2) His reign 13-15

3. The Rise of David and Decline ofSaul 16-31

4. The Kingdom of David 2 Samuel 1-24

    1) His success 1-10

    2) His sin and its consequences 1 1-20:22

    3) Conditions in his Kingdom 20:23-24:25

The Story

The book begins with the story of the birth and call of Samuel and the capture of the Ark by the Philistines. It progresses through the enthronement of Saul as king, his failure, and repudiation by Yahweh. The remainder of book one tells of God's choice of David, and his rise to prominence. Book 1 ends with the death of Saul. Book 2 begins with David's inauguration and establishment as king. God's covenant with David is highlighted in 2 Samuel 7. The remainder of book 2 tells of his sin and its consequences, the rebellion of Absalom, and a summary of his reign

Characteristics and Points of Interest

1. 1 & 2 Samuel were one book in the oldest Hebrew texts.

2. The book begins with Israel in great spiritual and political decline. It ends with the power of the Kingdom of David fully advanced.

3. The history of the book is usually but not always in chronological order.

4. Another Important theme is the monarchy

1) Its beginning – Though the motives of the people in wanting a king were wrong-they wanted to conform to the surrounding nations-a monarchy was in God's plan for his people.

2) Its results

   (1) Having a hereditary monarchy led to a -loss of the

      spontaneous leadership.

   (2) Centralization of power led to a loss of individual

      freedom.

   (3) A developing upper class - aristocracy surrounding

the kings led to economic inequity.

3) Its operation. The King is to rule for God. He is to be the Lord's servant administering the Lord's Kingdom. (However, Saul, a man, chosen because of his physical traits, never understood his position. Deuteronomy 17:14-20

5. A new name for God used in Samuel not used in Pentateuch. "Lord of Hosts"

6. God's covenant with David. 2 Samuel 7

7. The Rise of the prophetic office. The prophets were God's spokesmen and informed the King of God's will.

8. The ministry of the Holy Spirit in this new age. In a real sense the Kingdom marks a new way of God's governing. In Judges God ruled through the priests and judges. In Samuel he begins to rule through the kings and prophets.

9. Fulfillment of prophecies concerning Eli, Saul, and David.

10. Prophets named in Samuel are Samuel, Gad, and Nathan.

Major applications

1. The veracity of God. The book reports both the faith and the failures. Both the victories and the defeats. (e.g. of David 2:21, 27:1-19, 2 Samuel 11, 2 Samuel 24)

2. The consequences of sin in the lives of Gods people. (importance of obedience)

3. The ministry of the Holy Spirit in carrying out the work of God in raising up and empowering men to bring about his purpose and glory.

4. The importance of people in the outworking of the plan of God. If established men and missions do not carry out is work, God will establish new ones.

Recommended Resources

Robert D. Bergen, 1, 2 Samuel: An Exegetical and Theological Exposition, Holman, 1996

Dale Ralph Davis, 1 Samuel: Focus on the Heart, Christian Focus

Dale Ralph Davis, 2 Samuel: Out of Every Adversity, Christian Focus, 2013

John J Davis, The Birth of a Kingdom, Baker, 1970

*David Tsumura, The First Book of Samuel, (NICOT) Eerdmans, 2007

Ronald F. Youngblood, 1 & 2 Samuel, Zondervan, 2010

A Snapshot Of 1 & 2 Kings

Author

Unknown

Date of Events and Writing

From the Kingship of Solomon (971 B.C.) to the Babylonian Exile of Judah (560 B.C.). Probably written during the Exile.

Recipients

The Exiles

Theme

1 & 2 Kings are a divine evaluation of the Hebrew Kings. God blessed his obedient servants; He destroyed the disobedient.

Purpose

To demonstrate that the welfare of the nation depended on the faithfulness of its king to the Covenant Law (1 Kings 9:4-9) and to show the failure of the Hebrew Monarchy.

The Story

Kings begins with the establishment of the reign of Solomon including the building of the temple and Solomon's prosperity and failures. The rest of Kings details the events and kings of the divided kingdom. It tells of the exile of the northern kingdom of Israel by Assyria (722 B.C.) and that of Judah, including the destruction of Jerusalem in 586 B.C. ending with comments about Jehoiachin exiled in Babylon.

Outline

1. The United Kingdom under Solomon: Its rise (1:1-2:46), rule (3:1-4:34), Projects (5:1-9:25, Decline (9:26-11:40), and End 11:41-43.

2. The Divided Kingdom 1 Kings 12:1-2 Kings 17:11 (The separation of Israel from Judah)

3. The Single Kingdom of Judah. 18:1-25:30

Characteristics and Points of Interest

1. Kings is a Divine interpretation of the history of the Monarchy. Every king of Israel is evaluated as being evil. Some of the kings of Judah were considered good, but Judah became progressively worse.

2. Israel is the northern kingdom of the ten tribes whose capitals were Tirzah and Samaria. Judah is the southern two tribes of Judah and Benjamin reigned over by David's descendants at Jerusalem. Prominent among the good kings are Asa, Jehoshaphat, Jehoash (Joash), Hezekiah, and Josiah.

3. The author of Kings traces one kingdom's history until he gets chronologically beyond the other; then he switches.

4. Kings records the construction of the Temple 1 Kings 6-8

5. The sovereignty of God in Israel's history is a major emphasis of Kings. He blesses and chastens; He sends prophets and fulfills their words.

6. Judgment came because Israel's Kings failed to be true servants: neither obedient or dependent.

7. Not much is said about kings who were evil, even though some of these were politically significant. (Omri)

8. Kings records the second great period of miracles. The miraculous ministries of Elijah and Elisha were intended to repudiate the worship of Baal.

9. Prophets are key figures in Kings. Prominent among these are Nathan, Elijah, Elisha, and Isaiah.

10. All but three of the prophets whose books are found in the Old Testament ministered during this period of time.

Major Applications

1. No matter how great the man or how much he has done for God, he can still fail and experience God's chastening.

2. The patience, long-suffering, and mercy of God.

3. Earthly success does not impress God, only obedient faith.

4. In the most evil of times God still raises up faithful

witnesses for himself.

5. God will respond to a repentant heart regardless of the depth of previous wickedness.

6. The ministry of the godly can deter evil.

7. God is sovereign in human history.

8. God keeps His promises. (Davidic Covenant)

Recommended resources

Simon deVries, 1 Kings, Word 1985

H. R. Hobbs, 2 Kings, Word, 1985

Paul RT. House, 1, 2 Kings: An Exegetical and Theological Exposition, Holman, 1995

Iain Provan, 1 & 2 Kings, Hendrickson, 1993

J. Whitcomb, Solomon to the Exile, Baker, 1971

Chart of the Kings of Israel

Name	Dates	Evaluation	Enemies	Prophets
Jeroboam	931-910	Evil	Judah	Ahijah
Nadab	910-909	Evil	Judah	
Baasha*	909-886	Evil	Judah	Jehu
Elah	886-885	Evil		
Zimri*	885	Evil		
Omri*	885-874	Evil		
Ahab	874-853	Evil		Elijah Micaiah
Ahaziah	853-852	Evil	Moab	Elijah
Johoram	852-841	Evil	Moab/Syria	Elisha
Jehu*	841-814	Evil/Good		Elisha
Jehoahaz[b]	814-799	Evil		Elisha
Jehoash	799-782	Evil	Judah	Elisha
erboam	782-753	Evil	Syria	Jonah/Hosea /Amos
Zechariah	752	Evil		
Shallum*	751	Evil		
Menahem*	751-741	Evil	Assyria	

Pekahiah	742-740	Evil		
Pekah*[n]	751-731	Evil	Assyria	
Hoshea*	731-722	Evil	Assyria	

* Marks the beginning of a new family dynasty [b] Ahaziah and Jehoram were brothers [n] Pekah set up a rival kingdom in Gilead; he reigned in Samaria for 10 years (2 Kings 15:17, 27) [t] The first 5 kings of Israel ruled from Tirzah. Omri established Samaria as capital (1 Kings 16:24)

39

Chart of the Kings of Judah

Name	Dates	Evaluation	Enemies	Prophet
Rehoboam	931 - 913	Evil	Israel Egypt	Shemiah
Abijam	913 - 911	Evil	Israel	
Asa	911 - 870	Right	Israel	Hanani Azariah
Jehoshaphat[c]	873 - 848	Right*		Jehu/Eliezer/Jahaziel
Jehoram[c]	853 - 841	Evil	Edom/Libnah	Elijah
Ahaziah	841	Evil		
Athaliah[q]	841 -	Evil		

	835			
Joash	835 - 795	Right*		Joel Zechariah
Amaziah^c	796 - 767	Right	Edom Israel	
Azariah (Uzziah) ^c	790 - 740	Right*		Amos
Jotham^c	750 - 732	Right	Syria Israel	
Ahaz	732 - 715	Evil	Syria/Israel/Assyria	Isaiah Micah
Hezekiah	715 - 686	Right*	Assyria/Philistines	Isaiah
Manassah	687 -6	Evil*	Assyria	
Amon	642 -	Evil		

	640				
Josiah	640 - 609	Right	Egypt	Assyria	Huldah/Nahum/Zephaniah
Jehoahaz[b]	609	Evil	Egypt		Jeremiah
Jehoiakim[b]	609 - 598	Evil	Babylon		Habakkuk
Jehoiachin	598 - 597	Evil	Babylon		
Zedekiah[b]	597 - 586	Evil	Babylon		Obadiah

[b] brothers [c] co-regencies with their fathers

A Snapshot of 1 & 2 Chronicles

Author

Unnamed (Ezra is a good possibility)

Date of Events

From Adam to the return from the exile (mainly from David through the return) 538 B.C.

Date of Writing

Sometime after 538 B.C. @ 500 B.C. to 450 B.C.

Recipients

The returned remnant of the post-exile Jews.

Theme

God blesses His people through the godly line of David to whom He has given covenant promises.

Purpose

To rally the remnant to faithful temple worship by demonstrating God's covenant faithfulness and their link with the enduring promises made to David.

The Story

Chronicles traces the history of Israel from Adam to the edict of Cyrus to allow the Jewish exiles to return to their land (539 B.C.). Chronicles concentrates its attention on the reign of David and his descendants.

Outline

1. Background of the Monarchy 1:1-9:3

2. Rise of the Monarchy 9:35-29:30 "David"

3. Height of the Monarchy 2 Chronicles 1:1-9:31 "Solomon"

4. Decline of the Monarchy 10:1-36:21

5. Future of God's People 36: 22-23

Characteristics and Points of Interest

1. At the time of writing the people were discouraged, had a sense of failure and political obscurity and were doubting the value of their prescribed worship.

2. The Chronicler wanted to show:

   1) The significance of Israel as the people of the covenant.

   2) The importance of faithfulness to the covenant and in following the prescribed

rituals of worship at the temple.

3) The enduring promises of the Davidic Covenant.

3. Chronicles focuses on the Davidic line, and particularly on the blessings and victories. Omitted in Chronicles are such materials as: the reign of Saul, the exile of David under Saul, David's adultery, Absalom's rebellion, and the failures of Solomon. The Kings of Israel are only mentioned as they affect the Kings of Judah.

4. Chronicles also has an emphasis on the temple and temple worship.

5. The Davidic Covenant is also a key theme. 1 Chronicles 17: 11-14; 22:8-13; 28:6-7; 2 Chronicles 6:8-9, 16, 7:17-18; 13: 5; 21:7

6. God's selectivity is seen in the genealogies of 1 Chronicles 19, and the significance of the Davidic line and the Levitical family.

7. Chronicles is one book, first divided into 2 parts by the Greek translation (Septuagint)

Major Applications

1. The proper worship of the Lord.

2. Encouragement seen in the victories God gave to His loyal

followers.

3. Appreciation for one's spiritual heritage.

4. Hope in seeing the enduring promises of God

Recommended Resources:

Leslie C. Allen, and Adrian H. Curtis, <u>1 & 2 Chronicles</u>, T & T Clark, 2021

Mark Boda, <u>1-2 Chronicles</u>, Baker, 2019

*J.A. Thompson, <u>1,2 Chronicles</u> Holman, 1994

John C. Whitcomb, <u>Solomon to the Exile</u> Baker, 1971

A Snapshot of Ezra-Nehemiah

Author

Unstated, but some of it is the first-person record of Ezra. (Ezra 7-8) Nehemiah's memoirs are included in Nehemiah 1-8, 12:27-13:31. We do not know who compiled the book. Both Ezra and Nehemiah have been suggested.

Date of Events

From 538 B.C. to 420 B.C.

Date of Writing

@ 420 to 410 B.C.

Recipients

The returned exiles

Theme

God establishes His rule even during Gentile oppression.

1. God's sovereign working through Gentile rulers.

2. God' s faithful leaders

Purpose

1. To show how God sovereignly established the remnant in

the land of Canaan.

2. To Encourage trust in the Lord and faithful obedience.

The Story

Ezra-Nehemiah begins with the edict of King Cyrus allowing the Jews to return to rebuild the temple, the opposition they faced, the stoppage of the work for 16 years, its resumption and its completion in 515 B.C. The story moves on to the return of Ezra to Israel in 457 B.C. to organize the worship and deal with moral problems which had arisen. Nehemiah tells the story of Nehemiah migration to Israel to restore the walls of Jerusalem in 444 B.C. The book talks about challenges to the completion of the work and its completion.

Outline

1. The Temple Restoration. Ezra 1-6

2. The Reformation of Ezra. Ezra 7-10

3. The Restoration of the Walls. Nehemiah 1:1-7:3

4. The Reformation of Nehemiah. Nehemiah 7:4-13:31

The rest of Nehemiah tells of the renewal of the covenant, the dedication of the wall and the reforms of Nehemiah after came back a second time to serve as governor of the city.

Characteristics and Points of Interest

1. Ezra 4:8-6:18 and 7:12-26 are written in Aramaic, the diplomatic language of the time.

2. Ezra and Nehemiah were originally one book, not two.

3. Ezra 4 is not chronologically developed but is a thematic account of opposition under various kings.

4. The rebuilding of the Temple was under the leadership of Zerubbabel, a royal descendent of Jehoiachin, and Jeshua, a Levitical priest. [3:8-9]. Ezra did not arrive until some 58 years after the temple was completed.

5. Ezra was a priest and scribe whose purpose was to reestablish the Jewish Law and worship. He was given an official position by King Artaxerxes.

6. Nehemiah was appointed governor of Judah for the Persian state. Nehemiah 5:14. His purpose in coming (444 B.C.) was primarily Political: to rebuild the walls and make the city secure.

7. Zerubbabel and Jeshua were contemporary with Daniel. One wonders how much influence Daniel had on Cyrus' decision to let the Jews return to Jerusalem.

8. Nehemiah was contemporary with Malachi. Malachi may

have preached during Nehemiah's absence from Jerusalem from 432-420 B.C.

9. The book of Esther would seem to take place during the interval of time that elapsed between the rebuilding of the temple [515 B.C.] and the coming of Ezra to Jerusalem [457]B.C.).

10. Sequence of Events:

539/8 decree of Cyrus and return of the Jews to their land. Ezra 1:1

536 Foundations of the temple laid.

520 Resumption of construction following the preaching of Haggai and Zechariah. Ezra 4:24

515 Completion of the temple. Ezra 6:15

457 Coming of Ezra to Jerusalem. Ezra 7:1

444 Coming of Nehemiah to Jerusalem. 1:1, 2:1

432 Return of Nehemiah to Suza. Nehemiah 13:6, 5:14

?? Return of Nehemiah to Jerusalem. Nehemiah 13:6-7

410 Retirement of Nehemiah as governor according to Jewish tradition

Major Applications

1. God's work is accomplished by those who have zeal for His Word and for his work.

2. The necessity for ordering our lives by God's Word to accomplish his work.

3. The importance and characteristics of godly leadership.

4. The sovereignty of God

5. The importance of obedience, faithful prayer and diligent work to spiritual influence and success.

Recommended Resources

*T.J. Betts, Nehemiah: A Pastoral and Exegetical Commentary, Lexham, 2020

Mervin Breneman, Ezra, Nehemiah, Esther, Holman, 1993

F.Charles Fensham, The Books of Ezra and Nehemiah, (NICOT) Eerdmans, 1992

Derek Kidner, Ezra and Nehemiah, IVP, 1979

Gary V. Smith and Daniel L. Block, Ezra & Nehemiah: A Discourse Analysis of the Hebrew Bible, Zondervan, 2022

Charles Swindoll, Hand Me Another Brick, Bantam, 2007

A Chronological Chart of the Post-Exile Jewish People

539 B.C. Cyrus' [550 to 530 B.C.] edict allowing the Jews to return to their land. 2 Chronicles 36:22; Ezra 1:1

536 B.C. The restoration of the temple begun under Zerubbabel and Jeshua Ezra 3:8

536-520 B.C. Period of inactivity in the temple reconstruction Ezra 4:24

520 B.C. Prophetic preaching of Haggai and Zechariah Ezra 5: 1; Haggai l: l, Zechariah 1: 1

520 B.C. Temple reconstruction resumed Ezra 5:2

515 B.C. Temple reconstruction completed Ezra 6:15

500-450 B.C. Chronicles was probably written around this time

483 B.C. Esther became queen of Emperor Xerxes [486-464 B.C.].

472 B.C. The victory of the Jews in Suza over the plot of Haman. [Esther 3:7]

464-423 B.C. Reign of Artaxerxes I as king of the Persian

Empire.

457 B.C. Ezra's arrival in Jerusalem to establish the worship and Jewish legal system. [Ezra 7:1,7]

444 B.C. Nehemiah's arrival in Jerusalem to rebuild the wall of Jerusale. [Nehemiah 1:9]

432 B.C. Nehemiah's returned to Suza. Sometime later he came back to Jerusalem. [Nehemiah 5:14, 13:6]

420 B.C. The writing of Ezra-Nehemiah

550-330 B.C. The period of Persian rule. During this time the Jews were allowed to carry on their religious observances under the oversight of the Persian Satraps. The Jews were ruled by the High Priest who was responsible to Jewish governors appointed by the Persians.

A Snapshot of Esther

Author

Unknown

Date of Events

During the reign of the Persian King Xerxes (485-465 B.C.)
According to 1:3 the sequence of events began in his third
year @482 B.C.

Date of Writing

@ 450 B.C.

Recipients

The returned remnant.

Theme

The Sovereign God cares for and preserves his disobedient
people.

Purpose

1.To narrate the events which gave rise to the Jewish feast of
Purim.

2.To show how God preserved Israel even when they were
living outside His will.

3.To show that God is sovereign even when He seems to be silent.

The Story

The story begins with the events leading to the selection of the Jewess Esther to be the queen of the Persian emperor Xerxes. Esther's cousin Mordecai uncovers a plot against the king and eventually became the target of the jealous official Haman. In his wrath Haman deceived the king into signing an edict for the destruction of the Jews. With Mordecai's urging Esther agreed to appeal to the king in behalf of the Jewish people. While Haman was planning to kill Mordecai, the king instead directed him to publicly honor Mordecai for uncovering the assassination attempt. At a dinner with the king and Haman, Esther exposed Haman's plot and he was executed on the gallows he made for Mordecai. The king allowed the Jews to defend themselves and they defeated their enemies and instituted the feast of Purim in celebrate the victory. Finally, Mordecai is promoted to the rank of second in command under Xerxes.

Outline

1. Background: A Jewess Becomes Queen 1:1-3:15

2. Intrigue: A Plot Against the Jews 4:1-7:10.

3. Victory for the Jews 8:1-10: 3

Characteristics and Points of Interest

1. At the time of these events both Ezra and Nehemiah would have been in the Persian state.

2. There are no references to God or prayer in the Book of Esther. This omission is not accidental; it is intended to show the spiritual condition of Israel at this time

3. Esther and Mordecai are not shining examples of godly piety. They are never described as praying or consulting prophets or priests. Their actions are questionable. 2:12-15, 4:13-14, 3:2-4

4. Vashti's refusal seems justified, considering the motives of the King and his drunken guests.

5. Shushan (Suza) was one of four Persian capitals and due to its warm climate served as the winter capitol.

6. The gathering which led to the sequence of events in Esther is almost certainly the one in which Xerxes laid plans for his invasion of Greece.

Major Applications

1. God's promises will be fulfilled despite the failures of His people.

2. Satan's schemes (to destroy the Jews) will not succeed.

3. Success and prosperity are not always a sign of God's blessing and approval.

4. Salvation is a product of God's grace.

5. God is still at work when He seems to be silent.

6. The sin of living as though God were not necessary.

Recommended Resources

Sandra Berg, The Book of Esther: Motives, Themes and Structure, Scholars Press, 1979

Mervin Breneman, Ezra, Nehemiah, Esther, Holman, 1993

Timothy Cain, The God of Great Reversals: The Gospel in the Book of Esther, 2019

*Anthony Tomisino and H Wayne House, Esther, Lexham, 2016

John Whitcomb, Esther: Triumph of God's Sovereignty, Moody, 1979

A Snapshot of Job

Author

Unknown

Date of Events

Unknown. The story is old. Job seems to have lived in olden days, perhaps as far back as to the time of Abraham.

Date of Writing

Unknown.

Recipients

Unknown. Perhaps Israel. Perhaps during the exile.

Theme

The problem of pain in the life of the righteous.

Purpose

To show that those who suffer must learn to live by faith in the sovereign creator.

The Story

The story begins in heaven where Satan petitioned to God let him attack Job.

Though Satan mercilessly attacked Job, yet Job remained loyal to God. Job's three friends came to comfort him. After Job poured out his lament, his three friends attempted to convince him that these things had come upon him because of his sin. Thus, he needed to repent. Job countered their arguments by contending that he had not sinned, and that he was not being treated fairly by God. After three rounds of dialogue, a fourth man Elihu speaks up to rebuke both Job's friends and Job. He assured Job that God is just and mighty. The Lord himself speaks to Job showing him his majesty and power through the wonders of creation. Job then repented of his harsh words against God. The book ends with God confronting the three friends, Job's prayer for them and God's blessing of Job.

Outline

1. Introduction: The story 1:1 -3:26

2. Job's dialogue with his Three Friends. 4:1- 31:40

1) The first round 4:1-14:22

   (1) With Eliphaz (4-5) (Traditionalist) Job's response (6-7)

   (2) With Bildad (8) (Legalist) Job's response (9-10)

   (3) With Zophar (11) (Dogmatist) Job's response (12-14)

2) The second round 15:1-21:34 (Their accusations are more specific)

    (1) Eliphaz (15) Job's response (16—17)

    (2) Bildad (18) Job's response (19)

    (3) Zophar (20) Job's response (21)

3) The third round 22:1-26:14

    (1) Eliphaz (22) Job's response (23—24)

    (2) Bildad (25) Job's response (26)

4) Job's monologue 27-31

3. Elihu's speech 32

4. The proclamation of God 38:1-42:6

  1) God's first response 38:1-40:1

  2) Job's' response 40:3

  3) God's second speech 40:6-41:34

  4) Job's second response 42:1-6)

5. Conclusion 42:7-17.

  1) God's rebuke of the three friends. 42:7-9.

  2) God's blessing of Job. 42:6-17

Characteristics and Points of Interest

1. In Round 2 the charges against Job are more specific. In Round 3 the accusations are more emphatic.

2. The basic contention of the three friends: God is punishing you because you have sinned.

3. Job's complaint: I have not sinned. 27: 1 God, how can you treat me so unjustly?

4. Elihu's contention: God doesn't act unjustly. Who are you to accuse Him? 33:12-13, 34:5, 35:2, 36:2, 3

5. God's proclamation: I am the sovereign Lord of Creation. Trust me and do not accuse me or complain. God shows Job this power through the majesty of His creation

Major Applications

1. In suffering we are called to trust the Lord. We may not know why in this lifetime.

2. The danger of presuming that personal sin is always the reason for suffering.

3. The spiritual warfare taking place in heaven. We don't know what is happening.

Recommended Resources

Robert Alden, <u>Job</u>, Holman, 1994

* David Allen, <u>Exalting Jesus in Job</u>, Holman, 2022

John E. Hartley, <u>The Book of Job</u> [NICOT] Eerdmans, 1988

Tremper Longman, <u>Job</u>, Baker, 2016

A Snapshot of The Psalms

Author

David wrote around 73 of the Psalms. Other authors include: Moses - Psalm 90, Asaph - Psalm 50, 73-83, Sons of Korah- Psalm 42,44-49, 84, 85, 87, 88 Heman-Psalm 88, Ethan- Psalm 89, and Solomon Psalm 72, 127

Date of Writing

Varies according to the author. Psalms seems to have been compiled during the exile (Jewish tradition says Ezra was the compiler) between 586 and 516.

Recipients

The Jews of the exile and return.

Theme

The praise of God in the experiences of life. God is worthy of all praise. (Every Psalm except 88 has some element of praise) Purpose: To aid us in the praise and worship of God.

Outline

Psalms is composed of five distinct books.

1. Psalms 1-41

2. Psalms 42-72

3. Psalms73-89

4. Psalms 90-106

5. Psalms107-150

Some Bible scholars suggests that the Psalms were organized to reflect the Pentateuch, the first five books of the Old Testament. Others suggest that each book may have a predominant theme: 1-Mankind (Genesis), 2-Suffering (Exodus), 3-Holiness, worship (Leviticus), 4-Wandering and suffering (Numbers), 5-The Word (Law) of God (Deuteronomy). Others see no themes or progression of themes in or between the books.

Characteristics and Points of Interest

1. Psalms 1 & 2 serve as an introduction to the Psalms.

2. Each book of the psalms closes with a doxology: 41:13, 72:18-20, 89:52, 106:48 and Psalm 150 I which serves as the conclusion to the whole Psalter.

3. Psalms is the first Old Testament book of poetry. Hebrew poetry is a rhyming of ideas (various kinds are used) (Parallelism) rather than of words. (over 50% of the Old Testament is written in poetic language). There are several

types of parallelism including synonymous [the second line has the same meaning as the first line Example: Psalm 3:1], synthetic [the second line elaborates on the first line. Example: Psalm 40:2], climatic [the second line is the same as the first line except for the last words. Example: Psalm 29:1], emblematic [one line illustrates the other. Example: Psalm 42:1], antithetical [the second line is the opposite of the first line. Example: Psalm 1:6], and formal [No obvious connection between the two lines].

4. Poetic language of Psalms uses many figures of speech: metaphor (23: 1), simile (1:3), metonymy-a word is put for something connected with it (59:9), synecdoche -part for whole/whole for part. (Genesis 22:17), merism -gives the extremes to speak of everything between the extremes (Psalm 1:2,113:3).

5. Psalms is a hymnbook. The inspired superscriptions show that these poems were put to music. Elements included in the superscriptions include: the instruments (6), melody (45), occasion (92), type of poem (45), historical situation of the author (3) and the author's name (3)

6. Different kinds of Psalms have been cataloged:

1) Lament Psalms. (Personal and National) Example: Psalm 44 The Psalmist laments his situation. The format includes

most but not necessarily all of the following: (1) Address and opening to God, (2) Lament for one's situation, (3) Confession of trust in God, that He will deliver, (4) a Petition for deliverance, (5) A vow to praise God when He delivers. Example: Psalm 6.

2) Acknowledgement Psalms.

The Psalmist acknowledges God's answer to his prayer. They consist in the praise of God. Two types: (1) Declarative Praise. He declares God's deliverance. Example: Psalm 145, (2) Descriptive Praise. He describes his situation and how God delivered him. Example: Psalm 116, 117.

2) Petitionary Psalms. The psalmist beseeches God to answer his prayer. Example: Psalm 5

3) Imprecatory Psalms. In these Psalms the psalmist calls for God to pour out judgment on his enemies. Example: Psalm 58

4) Messianic Psalms.

The Psalm looks forward directly or indirectly to the coming of the Messiah.

(1) Directly speaking of Messiah. Example: Psalm 110, 22

(2) Having reference to a contemporary person but

indirectly fulfilled in Christ. Example Psalm 2

5) Alphabetical Psalms In these psalms each line or paragraph begins with a succeeding letter of the Hebrew alphabet. Examples: Psalm 34, 111, 119

7. Bible teachers have noted how various psalms echo other psalms or other Biblical texts. Psalm 14 and 53, Psalm 40:13-17 and Psalm 70, Psalm 57:7- 11 and 60:5-12 in Psalm 108, Exodus 34:6-7 in Psalm 86:15, 103:8, and 145:8, Numbers 6:24-26 in Psalm 31:16, 67:1, Psalm 80:3, 7, 19, 118:135.

Major Applications

1. To aid us in giving praise and worship to God.

2. To aid us in prayer. To teach us how to pray.

3. In coping with life, especially its problems and sufferings.

4. To build faith in God and His Messiah, Jesus Christ.

Recommended Resources

Ronald Allen, <u>And I Will Praise Him</u>, Nelson, 1999

C. Hassell Bullock, <u>Psalms</u>, 2 Vols. Baker, 2015, 2017

C. S. Lewis, <u>Reflections on the Psalms</u>, Harcourt, 1988

J. J. Stuart Perone, <u>Psalms</u>, Zondervan, 1966

*Allen P. Ross, <u>A Commentary on the Psalms</u>, Kregel, 2011

A Snapshot of Proverbs

Author

Solomon 1:1-9:18, 10:1-22:16, 25:1-29:27 (as copied by men of Hezekiah) Unnamed wise men (perhaps those mentioned in 1 Kings 4:31) 22:17-24:34 Agur 30, and Lemuel 31

Date of Writing

Perhaps compiled during the time of Hezekiah [715-686 B.C.)]

Recipients

Israel

Theme

The wisdom of the righteous life.

Purpose:

To teach people to live wisely and avoid unwise moral and social pitfalls. To teach people what wisdom consists of and to encourage people to live wisely.

Outline

1. Introduction 1:1-7

2. Ten Discourses of a Father 1:8-9:18

These chapters are not proverbs but an argument to persuade one to listen to the Proverbs to follow and to pursue wisdom.

3. Proverbs of Solomon 10:1-22:16

4. The Words of the wise 22:17-24:34

5. Proverbs of Solomon copied by the men of Hezekiah 25:1-29:27

6. The Words of Agur 30

7. The Words of Lemuel 31

Characteristics and Points of Interest

1. A proverb is a short pithy saying to govern living or to compare aspects of life based on observation. They are universal, individual and pragmatic. They are generalities and there may be exceptions to what the proverbs say is generally true.

2. Proverbs looks at many aspects of living: spiritual, moral, social, economics, civil government, personal relations, attitudes, actions, words, marriage, and family.

3. Chapters 1-9 are not "proverbs" as such, but an argument to persuade the reader to listen to the proverbs which follow.

4. Wisdom is not intelligence or education. It is skill in living

113

life in accordance to the principles of God's Word. It is skill in applying God's truth to everyday life. It is the proper grasp of the basic issues of life and of the relationship of God to man.

Major Applications

1.Proverbs gives us moral guidance in making wise decisions.

2. Proverbs teaches us how to live successfully in God's eyes and avoid unnecessary pitfalls.

3. Proverbs is a great textbook for teaching children about life.

Recommended Resources

*Robert L. Alden, <u>Proverbs: A Commentary on the Ancient Book of Timeless Advice,</u> Baker, 2019

Duane Garrett, <u>Proverbs, Ecclesiastes, Song of Solomon,</u> Holman, 1993

Derek Kidner, <u>Proverbs</u>, IVP, 2018

Tremper Longman III, <u>Proverbs</u>, Baker, 2015

Bruce Waltke, <u>The Book of Proverbs</u>, 2 volumes, [NICOT], Eerdmans, 2005

A Snapshot of Ecclesiastes

Author

Solomon. [1:1]

Date of Writing

Perhaps at the close of Solomon's life as he reflects on his life. Perhaps somewhere between 951and 931 B.C. It was after he had accumulated wealth and wisdom and had experienced life.

Recipients

Israel

Theme

Because life seems futile, man is wise to trust and obey God. Life apart from God is empty. The answer to life is not found in life but in God.

Purpose

To demonstrate that apart from God and his will life is vain. Thus, to motivate obedient faith. To convince the reader that since much of life cannot be fully understood, we must live by faith, enjoy the good things God gives us [2:24, 3:12-13, 22, 5:18, 19, 8:15, 9:7-9], and properly respond to God [fear

3:14, 5:7, 7:18, 8:12-13 12:13,] and his commands [obedience 2:26, 12:13]

Outline

1. The Theme Declared 1:1-11

2. The Theme Demonstrated 1:12-6:12

3. The Theme Developed 7:1-12:7

4. The Theme Concluded 12:8—14

Another way to see the book suggests a progression of thought. Each of the divisions ends with a conclusion about how life should be approached.

1. The frustrations of life. 1:2-2:26

2. Life as a God-ordered scheme. 3:1-5:20

3. Explanations of the inequities of life 6:1-8:15

4. Practical lessons for living. 8:1-12:8

5. Final conclusions 12:9-14

Characteristics and Points of Interest

The key word in the book is vanity (used 38 times). Cf. 1:2, 2:1, 11, 15, 17, 19, 21-23, 3:19, 4:4, 7, 8, 16, 5:10, 6:4, 9, 11, 12, 7:6, 8:10, 14, 11:8, and 12:8

1. The key text showing the purpose of the book is 12:13, 14.

2. Ecclesiastes examines life as it is experienced on earth. The goals for which men strive are futile.

3. Ecclesiastes shows that God is:

   1) Wise: Life, as it is, is His plan. 3:11

   2) Good: Life is His good gift to be enjoyed. 3:13

   3) A just judge to whom we must answer. 3:16, 17; 8:11-

      13, 11:9-10, 12:13-14

   4) Sovereign 3:14

4. Ecclesiastes sets forth the truth that life is an enigma-something that we just can't figure out. It appears to be a bad joke.

5. The main motivation Ecclesiastes give us to fear and obey God is the reality of judgment. 3:17, 9:1, 11:9, 12:14

Major Applications

1. Ecclesiastes is the book for the person who is puzzled by life.

2. Ecclesiastes is a book to help us when life doesn't make sense.

3. Ecclesiastes is a book to teach us the ultimate importance

of trust and obedience, no matter what life brings us.

4. Ecclesiastes is a book to teach us that life can be enjoyed as one who trusts and obeys God.

Recommended Resources

*Craig Bartholomew, Ecclesiastes, Baker, 2014

Daniel Fredericks and Daniel J Estes, Ecclesiastes and Song of Solomon, Apollos 2010

Tremper Longman III, The Book of Ecclesiastes, [NICOT] Eerdmans, 1998

Roy B. Zuck, Reflecting with Solomon, Wipf & Stock, 1994

A Snapshot of The Song of Solomon

Author

Solomon [1:1]

Date of Writing

During Solomon's life after he has become king. 1:12, @971-931

Date of Events

@ 971-931

Recipients

Israel

Theme

The marital love of Solomon and his Shulamite bride.

Purpose

To exonerate and celebrate the beauty of marriage as God's gift to mankind

The Story

The book begins with the reflections and anticipation of Solomon and his finance, their expressions of mutual love, and a fearful dream of the bride. Then we see Solomon arriving for the wedding and the wedding night.

Chapter 5 depicts the agony of being separated, of the joyous reunion when Solomon returns, and their meeting in a nut orchard. They yearn to be alone in the countryside and express their desires.

Outline

1. Preparation for the wedding. 1:1-3:5. "recollections"

1) Longings for affection. 1:1-8

2) Expressions of mutual love. 1:9-2:7

3) Pleasant memories. 2:8-17

4) A dream of separation. 3: 1-5

2. The wedding procession. 3:6-11

3. Perfection in marriage. 4-8

  1) The wedding night. 4:1-5:1

  2) The agony of separation. 5:2-6:3

  3) Solomon's return. 6:4-9

  4) In the nut orchard. 6:6:10-7:9

  5) Yearning to be alone in the country.7:10-8:4

6) Mutual expressions of love. 8:5-14

Characteristics and Points of Interest

1. The Song of Solomon is a book of Hebrew poetry. It consists of the poetic communication between Solomon and his Shulamite bride interspersed with responses of a choir called The Daughters of Jerusalem.

2. The Hebrew wedding depicted here consisted of three parts:

1)The Procession: The bridegroom went with his friends to the home of the bride to take her back with him to his home.

2)The Wedding Banquet (sometimes lasting 7 days)

3)The Physical Consummation

This is all following the legal agreement between the families, the marriage covenant. Malachi 2:14

3. The last two lines of 5:1 appear to be spoken by God as his approval of the physical love of the married couple.

4. A translation which distinguishes the words of Solomon and Shulamite is very helpful in reading the book with understanding.

5. Jews forbade the reading of the book until a man reached 30 years old.

6. Does The Song of Solomon have a typical meaning? This is possible. Some have suggested that it pictures: (1) The

relationship between God and Israel or (2) The relationship between Christ and the Church. These proposals are, at best, mere applications and not the proper interpretation of the book.

7. This important book exalts the institution of marriage and marital love.

8. The bride seems to have been a country, working class girl. The groom was a shepherd king.

Major Applications

1. To confirm clearly God's stamp of approval on physical love within the bonds of marriage. No one reading The Song of Solomon can justly say that the sexual relationship within marriage is dirty or a giving into lower animal instincts or unspiritual or carnal.

2. The support of the divine institution of marriage. The lovers of The Song of Solomon are a bridegroom and bride. They are not in an unmarried relationship.

3.To encourage Christian couples regarding the goodness and necessity of romantic and physical love within marriage.

Recommended Resources

Iain M. Duguid, The Song of Songs: Introduction and

Commentary, IVP 2015

Daniel Fredericks and Daniel J Estes, Ecclesiastes and Song of Solomon, Apollos 2010

*S. Craig Glickman, A Song for Lovers, IV Press, 1976

Richard Hess, The Song of Songs, Baker 2017

Tremper Longman III, Song of Songs, [NICOT], Eerdmans, 2001

Barry Webb, Five Festal Garments, IVP, 2000

A Snapshot of The Old Testament Prophetic Books

1. The nature of the Old Testament prophetic books

Old Testament prophetic literature is basically poetic. Thus, there is an extended use of figures of speech. It consists of both <u>predictive</u> and <u>declarative</u> elements. The prophets were the moral and spiritual leaders and preachers of Israel; therefore, even their predictions were intended to motivate God's people to righteous living.

2. The purpose of the prophetic books of Old Testament

1) Propetic literature is intended to teach truth about God and will.

2) Prophetric literature is intended to motivte faithfulness of God ad his will.

3) Prophetic literature is intended to, comfort and encourage the righteous.

4) Each propthetic book has it individual purpose in its historical setting.

5) Though there are prophecies directed toward Gentile

3. The scope of the prophetic books

Though there were prophets before Samuel, the rise of Samuel marked the beginning of the prophetic era and the prophetic books. [Deuteronomy 18:15, 18, Judges 6:8] Prophets spoke and wrote from the time of Samuel through the first generation of the New Testament church. The Old Testament prophetic books were written in the period of the Kingdoms of Israel and Judah and during and following the Exile. Malachi was the last of the prophets until John the Baptist.

1) The prophetic institution had its origin in God. The prophets spoke because God told them to speak.

2) The prophetic office was regulated by the Law. [Deuteronomy 131-20, 18:15-22]

3) The prophetic era basically began with the call of Samuel [Acts 3:24]. The need for this new era of prophetic spokesmen was found in:

(1) In the transition to a new way of God's ruling through kings which brought about a governmental pattern similar to the pagan Gentile states surrounding Israel; thus, there arose greater temptation to pattern religious and social life after the pagan Canaanites.

(2) In the fact that the priesthood was very corrupt as can be seen in Judges 17-19 and in the story of Eli's sons in 1 Smauel2. So, as the kingdom period began God raised up the prophets to proclaim his word. [1 Samuel 3:19-21, Amos 2:10-12 ,Acts 3:21] Prophetic schools or gilds also developed. [1 Samuel 10:5-10, 19:18-24, 2 Kings 2:1]

4) The prophetic era closed with the passing of the New Testament Apostolic generation. [Hebrews 2:3-4, Ephesians 2:20]

5) Jewish scholars divide the prophetic books into two parts: The Former Prophets, which we call the Historical Books and the Latter prophets, which we call the Major Prophets [Isaiah, Jeremiah/Lamentations, Ezekiel, and Daniel] and the Minor Prophets or The Twelve.

4. Keys to understanding biblical prophecy

1) A literal hermeneutic.

(1) A literal hermeneutic means that the words of Scripture are to be understood according to the normal laws of language and grammar.

(2) Words should be interpreted according to historical and cultural settings.

(3) Literal interpretation recognizes figures of speech and the use of allegory-but only when the contextual setting demands it.

(4) Literal interpretation calls for comparison of Scriptures. Scripture does not contradict itself.

(5) Literal interpretation recognizes the progressive nature of God's revelation. Matthew 10:1-6, Luke 10:1 [God did not reveal to Isaiah everything he revealed to John in the book of Revelation.]

(6) Each text of Scripture has only one God-intended meaning, though that meaning may be complex. It may have more than one application.

(7) If a literal meaning makes sense in its context, the text should be understood literally, unless there is good reason to believe otherwise. Some good reasons to accept a non-literal interpretation would be:

a. An interpretative key within the context. (Revelation 13:18).

b. If a literal interpretation would contradict other Scriptures. Ezekiel 28:12. [The King of Tyre cannot be the literal king of Tyre because of what is said about this person in v. 9-13.]

c. If the N.T. gives authority for a fuller meaning. Hosea 11:1, Matthew 2:15.

2) **Understanding the unique character of prophetic language.**

(1) In prophecy the future is predicted in terms of the prophet's own culture, vocabulary and experience, (e.g., battles with horses, spears, and arrows)

(2) The prophecy may be received and conveyed by different methods. Reception to the prophet: direct communication from God, dreams, visions, prophetic inspiration. Conveyance by the prophet: a direct message, parables [Ezekiel 23 - the two Sisters], [Isaiah 5-vineyard] or, symbolic actions [Ezekiel 4, 5, Jeremiah 13].

(3) The time element of prophetic speech may differ from ordinary speech.

a. A future event may be spoken of as being present or already completed. This is the prophetic perfect. [Isaiah 9:6-7, Numbers 24:17, Isaiah 5:13].

b. Two events, separated by a long period of time, may be brought together in one prophecy with no indication of the time lapse. [Daniel 9:26-27, Isaiah 61:1-2].

c. A prophecy may have a multiple fulfillment. It may have both a near fulfillment and a far fulfillment. [Isaiah 7:14] It may have a partial fulfillment and a later, total or full fulfillment. [Compare Joel 2:28-32 with Acts 2:17-21.]

4) Some prophecies are conditional, even though a condition may not be stated in the text. (Jonah's prophecy of the destruction of Nineveh)

5) The central theme of all prophecy is Christ and his Millennial Kingdom. Luke 24:27.

3) **Understanding the Biblical Covenants.**

(1) Definition: Biblical covenants are agreements which God makes with mankind.

(2) Types of covenants:

a. Conditional or bilateral. In these covenants both parties to the agreement bind themselves to certain responsibilities.

b. Unconditional or unilateral. In these covenants one party makes unconditional promises without putting obligations on the other party.

(3) The Biblical Covenants

a. **The Abrahamic Covenant**. Genesis 12-15.

a) Nature: unilateral/unconditional [Genesis 15:12-21]. That the covenant is unconditional does not mean that every succeeding generation would enjoy its benefits.

b) Participants: God and Abraham and his descendants through Isaac and Jacob.

c) Promises (a) the land of Canaan, (b) a seed, descendants, (c) a blessing which would extend to all nations.

d) Sign: circumcision. Genesis 17:1-14.

b. **The Mosaic Covenant**. Exodus 20 - Leviticus, Deuteronomy

a) Nature: conditional/bilateral.

b) Participants: God and the Nation of Israel.

Exodus24:8.

c) Promises: Blessing for obedience. Cursing for

disobedience.

d) Requirements: (a) Commands (governed moral life)

Exodus 19:3-20:26),

(b) Judgments (governed social life) Exodus 21:1-24:18),

and

(c) Ordinances (governed worship) Exodus 25:1-

Leviticus).

e) Sign: the Sabbath. Exodus 31:13-17.

c. **The Davidic Covenant**. 2 Samuel 7:1-17

a) Nature: Unconditional/unilateral.

b) Participants: God and David and his heirs.

c) Promises: Personal blessings (7:8-11a), an eternal kingship of David's heirs (7:11b-12, 16), an eternal kingdom over which his heirs would reign (7:13-16).

d. **The New Covenant**. Jeremiah 31:31-ff. Hebrews 8.

a) Nature: Unconditional/unilateral.

b) Participants: God and the Nation of Israel

c) Promises the national and spiritual restoration of Israel: Isaiah 59:20-21, Jeremiah 31:37, 40, 33:14-22, Ezekiel 36:24-28.

d) Sign: The Communion cup. Luke 22:20.

Note: Believers today enter the blessings of the New Covenant by faith in Jesus, whose death ratified the covenant and made the fulfillment of its promises possible. Luke 22:20, Hebrews 8.

All these covenants were made by God with Israel-not with the Gentiles or with the Church. Romans 9:1-4, Eph. 2:11-12.

e. Covenants in the ancient biblical world were usually ratified by means of a blood sacrifice. Genesis 15:7-19, Exodus 24:1-8, Luke 22:20, Hebrews 8:11-18

4) Recognizing the Distinction between Israel and the Church.

Israel was the Old Testament people of God. The Church is the New Testament people of God. Israel is not the Church. The Church is not Israel. The promises made to Israel will be fulfilled to Israel. The promises made to the Church will be fulfilled to the Church. There is a sense that in Jesus believers spiritually become the children of Abraham, and partake in the benefits of the New Covenant [Romans 4:16, Galatians 3:7-9, 14, 29] but that does not invalidate the promises made to Israel.

5. Focus of Old Testament Prophecy

Though every Old Testament prophecy is not about Jesus, Old Testament prophecy leads to Jesus, his birth, his ministry, his atoning death, his resurrection, his ascension and his return to reign in his eternal kingdom.

6. The chronological order of the Prophetic books

Dating the ministries of the prophets and the dates of the writing of their books is not an exact science. Some of the books may have been edited or arranged by others. However, helpful information for dating some of the ministries and books can be found in the names of current enemies and foreign kings referred to in the book and in the mention or silence about well-known political events. Some of the prophets give us the perimeters of their ministries by mentioning the kings of Israel or Judah reigning during their ministries. [e.g. Isaiah 1:1] Most of the dates below should be prefaced with an @

Prophet	Time of Ministry	Date of Writing
Joel	830 B.C. to 800 B.C.	800 B.C.
Amos	765 B.C. to 750 B.C.	750 B.C.
Jonah	780B.C. to 760 B.C.	730 B.C.
Hosea	760 B.C. to685 B.C.	715 B.C.
Micah	735 B.C. to 720 B.C.	700 B.C.
Isaiah	740 B.C. to 680 B.C.	680 B.C.

Nahum	650 B.C. to 630 B.C.	630 B.C.
Zephaniah	640 B.C. to 620 B.C.	620 B.C.
Habakkuk	609B.C. to 605 B.C.	605 B.C.
Obadiah	586 B.C.	586 B.C.
Jeremiah	625 B.C. to 585 B.C.	580 B.C.
Ezekiel	593 B.C. to 571 B.C.	570 B.C.
Daniel	605 B.C. to 536 B.C.	530 B.C.
Haggai	520 B.C. to 515 B.C.	510 B.C.
Zechariah	520 B.C. to 470 B.C.	470 B.C.
Malachi	432 B.C. to 420 B.C.	420 B.C.

Recommended Resources

*Hobart Freeman, An Introduction to the Old Testament Prophets, Moody, 1968

J. Dwight Pentecost, Things to Come, Zondervan, 1958

John F. Walvoord, The Prophecy Knowledge Handbook, Victor, 1990

Edward J. Young, My Servants, the Prophets, Eerdmans, 1952

A Snapshot of Isaiah

Author

Isaiah, son of Amoz, from Jerusalem [1:1]

Date of Ministry

@ 740-701. Book compiled after 686 B.C. [1:1]

Recipients

Judah

Theme

The salvation of the Lord. The holy God will chasten His people to prepare them for His program of salvation of all peoples.

Purpose

To remind Judah of the special relationship they had with God to turn them back to a proper covenantal relationship with God to encourage the righteous to trust in God and to give hope.

The Story

Isaiah's story begins with his call to prophetic ministry in 740 B.C. [6:113]

Only two of his prophecies are dated. [7:1, 20, 36:1] The only chapters which include narrative are chapters 6, 7, 8 and 36-39. Chapters 36-39 tell the story of what happened when Sennacherib, king of Assyria invaded Judah in 701 B.C. during the reign of Hezekiah king of Judah and Hezekiah's interaction with Isaiah over this crisis. This story ends with the destruction of the Assyrian army besieging Jerusalem and the assassination of Sennacherib. Two other incidents from the life of Hezekiah are recorded. The first incident is his illness and recovery and God's promise of fifteen more years of life. The second is Hezekiah's unwise disclosure of his wealth to some Babylonian envoys leading to the prophecy that Jerusalem's treasures would be taken to Babylon.

Outline

1. The Prophetic Condemnation 1-35

   Of Judah 1-12

   Of the Gentile Nations 13-23

   Universal judgment and blessing 24-35

2. The Historical Interlude 36-39 (validates 1-35)

3. The Prophetic Consolation 40-66

Restoration Proclaimed 40-57

Restoration Confirmed 58-66

The Deliverance 40-48

The Deliverer 49-57

The Delivered 58-66

Characteristics and Points of Interest

1. There is a distinct change of focus between chapters 1-39 & 40-66 from condemnation to deliverance, but this does not suggest a different author as the liberals say.

2. The servant songs 42-53 find their ultimate fulfillment in Jesus Christ.

3. Isaiah is a very literary, poetic, and colorful book and longest of the prophets.

4. Isaiah seems to have been a court preacher, a prophet to the kings.

5. Isaiah's life and children are a part of his message.[7:3, 8:3, 18, 20:3]

5. 2 Chronicles 32:32 seems to refer to Isaiah 36-39 and may imply that Isaiah was, in part, the author of 1 & 2 Kings.

6. Isaiah is much quoted in the New Testament. He is

mentioned by name 22 times.

7. Isaiah has been called the Gospel of the Old Testament. It predicts the birth of Jesus [7:14, 9:6-7], his ministry [61:1-4], his death [52:12-53:12], his resurrection [53:10], and his kingdom reign [2:1-4, 9:1-7, 11:1-16, 59:20

8. Isaiah is full of many outstanding prophecies.

9. Isaiah gives us one of the few biblical descriptions of the presence of God, [6:1-13], which is also Isaiah's call and commission. Other descriptions are found in Exodus 33:18-23, Ezekiel 1, Revelation 1, 4 and 5

10. Some of Isaiah's major themes are the remnant, the coming kingdom, peace, joy, justice and the Suffering Servant.

Major Applications

1. To give us assurance and hope. The Sovereign Lord has a plan (Salvation) that he will accomplish. Isaiah 55:6-13

2. To show us the Greatness of God. Isaiah 44:6, 43: 10, 11

3. To show the foolishness of idolatry 44:12-17

4. To teach us about serving God. 6

5. To affirm the centrality of Christ, the suffering servant and coming King.

6. To call us to hope, trust, and obedience to the Lord.

7. Remarkable prophecies to affirm the truthfulness of Scripture.

Recommended Resources

Trent Butler & Max Anders, Isaiah, Holman, 2002

*Paul R. House, Isaiah 1-27, Isaiah 28-66, Mentor, 2018

Alec J. Motyer, The Prophecy of Isaiah, IVP, 1998

John N. Oswalt, The Book of Isaiah,[2 volumes], [NICOT] Eerdmans, 1998

Gary V. Smith, Isaiah: An Exegetical and Theological Exposition, Holman, 2009

Alan B. Stringfellow, Insights on the Book of Isaiah, Whitaker House, 2019

Warren Wiersbe, Be Comforted, David C. Cook, 2009

Edward J Young, The Book of Isaiah, [3 Vols] Eerdmans, 1968

A Snapshot of Jeremiah

Author

Jeremiah [1:1] Jeremiah gave the prophecies. Who compiled them is unknown.

Date of Ministry and Writing

Jeremiah ministered from the reign of Josiah [1:2] until after the captivity began, [1:3] [627-585 B.C.] The book was compiled after 585 B.C.

Recipients

The Judean Exiles

Theme:

A Warning of Judgment

Purpose

 To explain to the Judean exiles why the judgment which had come and to give them a reassuring word of certain restoration.

The Story

Jeremiah was called into his prophetic by God in 627 B.C. the thirteenth year of the reign of good king Josiah of Judah

(640-609). He continued his prophetic mission through the last five kings of Judah until after the fall of Jerusalem to Babylon in 586 B.C. Jeremiah called Judah to mourn the death of Josiah when Josiah was killed in his ill-fated attempt to aid the Assyrians against Egypt. [2Kings 23:28-30, Jeremiah 22:10]. The first reference to opposition to Jeremiah comes from some men from his hometown who threatened his life.[11:21] Jeremiah predicted the exile of Josiah's son Jehoahaz to Egypt after only a three-month reign [Shallum] [22:11-12].

At the beginning of the reign of Jehoiakim [609-597] Jeremiah was surrounded by hostile people including priests and false prophets who sought to kill him. He was delivered by court officials led by Ahikam [26:1-24]. Their complaint was his prophecy of the downfall of Jerusalem. Another event during the reign of Jehoiakim was Jeremiah's use of the Rechabite sect as a prophetic sign [35:1-19].

One notable was the burning of Jeremiah's prophetic scroll by king Jehoiakim [36:1-26] and the subsequent curse upon the line of Jehoiakim [36:27-31] In 598 B.C. Jehoiakim was taken captive by the Babylonians and died on his way to exile. According to tradition Nebuchadnezzar had his body dumped outside the wall of Jerusalem as Jeremiah had predicted. [22:18-19]

Jeremiah 24 records a prophecy which took place in the very short reign of Jehoiachin [597] the son of Jehoiakim.

At the beginning of the reign of Zedekiah [597-586] Jeremiah was confronted at the temple by a false prophet, Hananiah who broke the ox yoke Jeremiah was using as an object lesson. This confrontation ended with Jeremiah predicting Hananiah's death which took place within the year. [28:1-17]

Another event which probably took place early in Zedekiah reign was the persecution of Jeremiah by Pashhur a chief official of the temple, who had Jeremiah beaten and placed in stocks. [20:1-6]. Chapter 29 records a letter sent by Jeremiah to the exiles in Babylon in response to letters sent from Babylon by Shemaiah.

As the fall of Jerusalem drew near the opposition to Jeremiah grew. The progression of events is not completely clear. First, Jeremiah was imprisoned and charged with deserting to the besieging Babylonians and thrown into a dungeon. King Zedekiah had him taken from the dungeon and placed in house arrest in the palace. [37:21]. During this time Jeremiah, though imprisoned, bought a field in his hometown [32:1-16]. In chapter 38 Jeremiah is thrown into

143

a muddy cistern. King Zedekiah had his feeble body lifted from the cistern and returned him to house arrest. During the siege King Zedekiah sought out Jeremiah several times for prayer and advice. [21:1-14, 37:3, 7, 38:14-16, 24]

When Nebuchadnezzar took Jerusalem he killed Zedekiah's son in Zedekiah's presence then put out his eyes and took him to Babylon [39:1-10] At Nebuchadnezzar's command he offered to release Jeremiah and put him the care of Gedaliah, who was appointed governor of Judah. Nebuzaradan, the Babylonian commander offered to take Jeremiah to Babylon, but Jeremiah decided to remain with Gedaliah. [40:1-6]. When Gedaliah was murdered Jeremiah and his secretary Baruch were taken to Egypt with a band of rebels fleeing Judah, in spite of Jeremiah's assurance that they could safely stay in Judah. [42:1-22] Jeremiah continued his prophetic ministry in Taphanhes, Egypt. As far as we know he died in Egypt.

Outline:

1. Introduction 1: 1-19

  1) The Prophet 1:1-3

    (1) The Call of the Prophet 1:4-8

    (2) The Commission of the Prophet 1:9-10

(3) The Content of his Messages 1:11-19

2. Jehovah's Words of Contention and Rejection 2-20

1) His Words of Contention 2-12

(1) The charge of faithlessness 2:1-6:30

(2) The charge of deceiving words 7:1-10:45

(3) The verdict 11:1-12:17

2) His Words of Rejection 13-20

(1) The message of the ruined waistband 13:1-27

(2) The message of the drought 14:1-15:21

(3) The message of the prophet's life 16:1-17:18

(4) The message of the public gate 17:19-27

(5) The message of the pottery 18:1-19:15 ·

3. Jehovah's Messages of Certain Judgment from the North 21-39

1) Prophetic words of Judgment 21-25

(1) Declaration of imminent judgment 21:1-14

(2) Messages to the kings of Judah 22:1-23:8

(3) Messages concerning the prophets 23:9-40

(4) Message of the figs 24:1-10

(5) Message for all the people 25:1-38

2) Prophetic experiences of Judgment 26-29

   (1) Message of the courtyard 26:1-24

   (2) Messages of the yoke 27:1-29:32

 3) Messages of Consolation 30-33

 4) Responses to the Message of Judgment 34-39

4. Messages to the Remnant 40-45

Continued rejection of the word and continued judgment

5. Messages to the Nations 46-51

The nations addressed are arranged geographically. There are 9 messages.

6. Conclusion: The Fall of Jerusalem in detail 52

Characteristics and Points of Interest:

1. Jeremiah is one of the most personal of the prophetic books. A lot of his experiences and his personal confessions are interspersed with the prophecies. He is the weeping prophet.

2. The development of the book is not primarily

146

chronological.

3. The climax and emphasis of the book is the fall of Jerusalem. (1-38) looks toward that event, (39) records it, (40-51) in light of that event, (52) restates it in detail.

4. Jeremiah was contemporary with Nahum, Habakkuk, Zephaniah, Daniel and Ezekiel.

5. Jeremiah 31:31-34 is the important announcement of the New Covenant.

6. Jeremiah, like many of the prophets was rejected and persecuted. 11:19 11:21-23, 18:18, 20:1-2, 26:8-11, 37:11-21, 38:4-13, 43:1-6.

7. We are told in 2 Chronicles 35:25 that Jeremiah gave the eulogy for Josiah.

Major Applications

1. The need to care. Jeremiah was not detached from his message; he felt it—the weeping prophet.

2. No one is above the Word of God - no priest, prophet, or nation.

3. Ignoring God's Word will prove disastrous.

4. The sovereignty of God

5. The judgment and mercy of God. Its certainty.

6. Encouragement for the remnant - God wants his children to understand he is active in the world though they may not

understand what he is doing at the present time.

7. Trustworthiness of God's word.

8. The cost of proclaiming God's truth.

9. The reward of faithfulness - Jeremiah was a priest in a small village at the time of his prophetic call.

Recommended Resources

Terence Fretheim, Author, 2002

F. B. Huey, Jeremiah, Lamentations, Holman, 1993

*Walter Kaiser, and Tiberius Rata, Walking the Ancient Paths, Lexham, 2019

Hetty Lalleman, Jeremiah and Lamentations, IVP, 2013

J. A. Thompson, The Book of Jeremiah [NICOT] Eerdmans, 1980

Christopher J. H. Wright, The Message of Jeremiah, IVP, 2014

A Snapshot of Lamentations

Author

Unstated in the text but tradition uniformly says: Jeremiah. (cf. also 2 Chronicles 35:25) (The author was one who had personally experienced the destruction of Jerusalem. Lamentations 3:53, 54 may imply Jeremiah's experience recorded in Jeremiah 38.

Recipients

The Judean Exile

Date of Writing

After the destruction of Jerusalem in 586 B.C.

Theme

A lament over the destruction of Jerusalem. (Sub-themes: confession, mercy, and hope in God's faithfulness)

Purpose

1. To provide a full, yet controlled, expression of grief for the exiles.

2. To spur the exiles to confession and repentance.

3. To rebuild their trust and confidence in the goodness,

power and mercy of the Lord

The Story

Lamentations is not story per se. It is a lament over the destruction of Jerusalem and its temple by the Babylonians and the exile of its people to Babylon in 586 B.C.

Outline

1. A lament for the distress of Jerusalem (1)

2. The Judgment of Jerusalem is for sin (2)

3. A Personification of suffering by the prophet (3)

4. The suffering of the City (4)

5. A prayer for God to remember their suffering (5)

Characteristics and Points of Interest

1. The structure of the book consists of five poems. The first four are acrostics (e.g. each verse begins with a succeeding letter of the Hebrew alphabet until all 22 letters are used.

In chapter 3, three verses in a sequence starting with the same letter. Chapter 5 is not an acrostic, but still contains 22 verses. Why is this structure used? (1) As an aid to memorization. (2) To express the idea of fullness of expression. (Grief is expressed from A to Z (Aleph to Tau)

(3) To limit the expression of grief— this is not irrational grief, but controlled and limited expression of it.

2. The physical pain the people experienced was not nearly so severe as the emotional and spiritual trauma — God's people exiled, the temple destroyed, and the nation collapsed.

3. In the midst of this grief is an unyielding faith and a sincere confession.

   Chapters 1,2,3 end with prayer, chapter 5 is a prayer.

4. There was at this time, popular doubt as to God's power.

   The pagans would say that the destruction of Jerusalem was because their gods were stronger than Israel's God.

5. Both the cause [sin] and the remedy for the situation [repentance] are clear cause- 1:5, 8,9,12,18,2:24, 3:39, 4:6, cure - 3:40, 4:22

6. This book was publicly read by the Jews on the anniversary of the fall of Jerusalem.

7. The outlook of the book is sometimes personal (use of pronoun "I") and sometimes national (pronoun "we")

Major Applications

1. The consequences of sin -There is a need to consider the consequences of our actions. 1:5, 8, 9, this disaster is clearly an act of judgment. 2:1-8, 17

2. The need to confess our sins.

3. The importance of expressing grief over sin and its consequences, a full but controlled expression.

4. In the darkest of times there is always hope in the faithful God , expressed in prayer.

5. The need to turn to God in prayer in times of grief and despair.

6. Having a heart for those who suffer 2:11, 3:48, 49.

7. Faith in the Lord need not be weakened by pain and suffering, but indeed may purify and strengthen it. James 1:2-4

8. How to survive national disaster without falling into personal despair. God is not any less sovereign, loving or faithful in times of disaster than as in times of prosperity. We need never doubt God's power and goodness.

9. Lamentations provides us with an example of how to express our grief.

It is not wrong to express grief as well as to express hope and confess sin.

Recommended Resources

Duane Garrett and Paul House, <u>Song of Songs & Lamentations</u>

F. B. Huey, <u>Jeremiah Lamentations</u>, [NAC] Holman

Norman K. Gottwald, <u>Studies in the Book of Lamentations</u>, SCM Press, 1962

*Barry G. Webb, <u>Five Festal Garments</u>, IVP, 2000

Christopher J. H. Wright, <u>The Message of Lamentations</u>, IVP, 2015

A Snapshot of Ezekiel

Author

Ezekiel was a priest (1:3) who was taken captive to Babylon by Nebuchadnezzar in 597 b c. 2 Kings 24:10-16, Jeremiah 29:1-2

Date of Writing

After 570 B.C.

Date of Events

592 B.C. (1:2) to 570 B.C. (29:17)

Recipients

The Jewish Exiles 11 :25

Theme

The purpose of the captivity is the purging of Israel for the glory of God.

Purpose

To keep before the exiles the sins which were the grounds of Israel's punishment and to encourage the faithful remnant with the prospect of restoration. (A two-sided purpose, both negative and positive. 14:21-23)

The Story

In 592 B.C. Ezekiel received his prophetic call through a dramatic vision of God while he was in exile in Babylon.[1] His last prophecy is dated in 570 B.C. [29:17]

Ezekiel was among the captives taken to Babylon in 597 B.C. By his words and symbolic acts Ezekiel communicated God's messages of judgment and future restoration of Israel. Twice we are told that Ezekiel's prophetic word was a response to an inquiry of the Jewish elders in exile. [8:1, 20:1] As far as we know Ezekiel died in Babylon

Outline

1. Vision of God's Glory 1

2. God's Glory in the Events of History 2-32

   1) Condemnation of Judah 2-24

   2) Condemnation of the Gentile Nations 25-32

3. God's Glory in Future Events 33-48

   1) Restoration of Israel's Nation 33-39

   2) Restoration of Israel's Worship 40-48

Characteristics and Points of Interest

1. In Ezekiel God uses many methods of revelation. The prophet himself is a message (through his actions and life experiences -including the death of his wife. (cf. chapters 4, 5, 9, 21, 24) Other methods: visions (7), direct addresses, parables/analogies (15-vine, 1- harlot, 17-eagles, 23-two sisters)

2. Chapters 1-24 are generally chronological. 25-48 are generally topical.

3. Noteworthy chapters: (1) Vision of God[ ]1, (2) Satan's fall [28], (3) Restoration of the Jewish nation [36], and (4) The defeat of Gog and his allies. [38-39]

4. The restoration of the temple priesthood, sacrifices is literal & millennial. The Old Testament sacrifices were prospective (looked forward to Christ) millennial sacrifices are memorials (look back to Christ)

5. Ezekiel was contemporary with Jeremiah (Jeremiah 9:1-2) and Daniel.(14: 14).

6. Key phrases: 1. The glory of God. 2. You or they shall know that I am the Lord. (used over 60 times.)

7. Ezekiel is often addressed as Son of man. [95 times]

Major Applications

1. The utmost value of the glory of God.

2. The indescribable glory of the God that we worship.

3. God's justice is always with just cause.

4. Our hope in the Lord, not in armies or personal attainment.

5. God wants us to know Him truly.

Recommended Resources

* Charles Lee Feinberg, The Prophecy of Ezekiel, Moody Press, 1969

Daniel I. Block, The Book of Ezekiel, 2 Volumes, [NICOT] Eerdmans, 1997

Iain M. Duguid, Ezekiel, Zondervan, 1999

Christopher J.H. Wright, The Message of Ezekiel, IVP, 2001

A Snapshot of Daniel

Author

Unstated. Chapters 7-12 are written by Daniel (1st person account) We don't know who compiled the book. It might have been Daniel.

Daniel, who was from the higher strata of of Judah was taken captive to Babylon by Nebuchadnezzar in 605 B.C. There were three deportations: (1) 605 B.C.- Daniel, (2) 597 B.C.- Ezekiel and (3)586 B.C.-Jerusalem destroyed.

Date of Ministry

Daniel's ministry as covered in this book runs from 606 B.C. to 536 B.C.

Date of Writing

@ 530 B.C.

Recipients

The remnant of the exiles at the time of and after the return.

Theme

The sovereignty of God over the world powers.

Purpose:

To give the Jews hope during the times of Gentile world dominion.

The Story

In 605 B.C. Daniel was among a number of royal and elite young Jews who were taken captive to Babylon. After a time of training Daniel and the others were placed in governmental service under the Babylonian king. The chapter shows Daniel and his three associates' faithfulness to God and God's law and God's intervention on their behalf. Daniel continued in that governmental service until 539. B.C. the year when Cyrus defeated the Babylonians and established the Medio-Persian Empire. Daniel had the opportunity to interpret two prophetic dreams given to King Nebuchadnezzar (605-562 B.C.)

Chapter 2 is Nebuchadnezzar's prophetic dream of the great image depicting the succession of world empires until the rise of God's eternal kingdom. Chapter 3 relates the story of three of Daniel's Jewish associates who were thrown into a furnace of fire for refusing to worship an image of the king and miraculously spared. Chapter 4 is the account of Nebuchadnezzar's period of insanity unveiled in a dream Daniel's interpreted. Chapter 5 relates the story of a divine prediction of the fall of Babylon given through handwriting on a wall during the reign of Belshazzar (553-539 B.C.) and interpreted by Daniel.

Chapter 6 records the story of Daniel being thrown into a den of lions but delivered by God, which took place in the first year of the reign of a Persian ruler named Darius (6:28), who may have been a provincial governor of Babylon, named Gubaru in the ancient Persian records. Some suggest the name Darius here could be an alternative name for the Emperor Cyrus.

The rest of the book records various prophetic dreams and visions given to Daniel about the progression of Gentile dominion until the coming of the kingdom of the messianic Son of Man (7:13-14).

Daniel continued in governmental service until 539 B.C. (1:21, 6:28).

His last prophecy recorded comes from 536 B.C. (10:1) As far as we know Daniel died in Persia.

Outline

1. Historical Introduction 1:1 - 21

2. The Nations of the world: their character, relation to

160

Israel, succession, and destiny. 2:1-7:28

  1) The Image Dream of Nebuchadnezzar 2

  2) The Fiery Furnace 3

  3) The Humiliation of Nebuchadnezzar 4

  4) The Feast of Belshazzar 5

  5) Daniel and the Lion's Den 6

  6) The Vision of the Four Beasts 7

3. The Nation of Israel: Their relation to Gentile dominion and future in the plan of Go 8:1-12:13

1) Vision of the Goat and its Horn 8

2) Daniel's prayer and the prophecy of the 70 weeks 9

3) Vision of the angelic messenger 10

4) Vision of the battles of the kings 11-12

Characteristics and Points of Interest

1. Daniel is full of visions, dreams, and angelic messengers.

2. The focus of 2:4-7:28 is on the Gentiles, thus it is written in Aramaic the main Gentile trade language of Daniel's time. The rest of the book focuses on the Jews and is written in Hebrew.

3. The stories, chapters 1, 3, 4, and,6 teach doctrinal truth related to the theme of the book.

4. Chapters 2 and 7 give us a prophetic schedule reaching from Babylon to the reign of Christ.

5. Daniel 9:24-27 is one of the most important and precise prophecies of the Old Testament. 6. Note: Daniel's awareness of earlier prophetic scriptures in Daniel 9:2 and Jeremiah 25:11-12.

7. Daniel was contemporary with Obadiah, Jeremiah, and Ezekiel.

8. Daniel is mentioned by name in Ezekiel 14:20, 28:3, and Matthew 24:15. He is indirectly mentioned in Hebrews 11:3

9. Chapter 8 is a prophecy of the defeat of the Medio-Persians by Alexander and the Greeks.

10. Chapters 10-11 are an incredibly detailed prophecy of the history which transpired during the Greek Era involving the Ptolemaic Dynasty of Egypt and the Seleucid rulers of Syria. Most significant in this was the reign of Antiochus Epiphanes (174-163 B.C.) (11:21-35) whose autocracies and desecration of the temple in 168 B.C. in led to the Maccabean revolt.

11. The little horn of Daniel 7 and the willful king of 11:36-45 would seem to be prophecies of the one the New Testament will call the Antichrist (1 John 2:18), Man of Lawlessness (2 Thessalonians 2:3), and the Beast (Revelation 13).

12. Daniel 12:2 is one of just a few Old Testament texts which directly speaks about the resurrection of the dead.

Major Applications

1.God is sovereign over human affairs, human governments and nations.

2. God blesses and uses the faithful among His children even in times of distress and captivity.

3. No earthly power can overcome God and those He chooses to protect or prevent the destruction of those who he determines to overthrow.

4. How godly men should pray and seek God's wisdom.

5. Hope for the people of God

Recommended Resources

Joyce G. Baldwin, <u>Daniel: An Introduction and Commentary</u>, IVP, 2016

Alva McClain, <u>Daniel's Prophecy of the Seventy Weeks</u>, BMH, 2007

Renald Showers, <u>The Most High God</u>, Friends of Israel, 1982

John F. Walvoord, <u>Daniel: The Key to Prophetic Revelation,</u> Moody, 1971

*Leon J. Wood, <u>A Commentary on Daniel</u>, Wipf & Stock, 1973

A Chronology of the Times of Daniel

626 B.C. The New Babylonian dynasty is established by Nabopolassar (626-605), the father of Nebuchadnezzar.

612 B.C. The Fall of the Assyrian capital of Nineveh to the Babylonians.

609 B.C. Josiah, king of Judah from 640-609 is slain trying to prevent the Egyptian army from contesting the Babylonians. 2 Kings 23 :29, 2 Chronicles 35:20-27

609 B.C. Jehoahaz, Josiah's son reigns over Judah for 3 months. He is taken captive to Egypt. 2 Kings 23:30-34, 2 Chronicles 36:1-4

609 B.C. Eliakim, son of Josiah is put on the Judean throne by the Egyptian ruler and renamed Jehoiakim. He reigned until 597 B.C. 2 Kings 23:34-37, 2 Ch. 36:5-8

605 B.C. Egypt is defeated by the Babylonians under the leadership of crown prince, Nebuchadnezzar at Carchemish. The Babylonians begin to take control of the Syrio-Palestinian region. [2 Kings 24: 7] At this time Nebuchadnezzar came to Jerusalem and captured Jehoiakim and then released him. He also took spoil and a number of captives including Daniel back to Babylon.2 Kgs 23:36-

24:72 Ch 36:5-8, Daniel 1:1-2, Nebuchadnezzar (605-562) returned to Babylon at the death of his father to be enthroned.

597 B.C. Jehoiachin, son of Jehoiakim, became king of Judah for 3 months. He was then deported to Babylon with a number of others including Ezekiel, 2 Kings 24:15-16, 2 Chronicles 36:9-10, Ezekiel 1:1-2

597 B.C. The Babylonians appoint Mattaniah, a son of Josiah, as Judean king and change his name to Zedekiah. 2 Kings 24:17-20, 2 Ch.36:10-14, Jeremiah 37: I

586 B.C. Zedekiah is captured and deported. Jerusalem and its temple are destroyed. Many others are taken away to Babylon. [2 Kings 25:1-21, Jeremiah 39, 52, 2 Chronicles 36:15-21]

581 B.C. More Judeans are taken away to Babylon.

562 B.C. Nebuchadnezzar died and his son Amel-Marduk (Evil-Merodach) (562-560) began to reign. He was assassinated by his successor.

560 B.C. Jehoiachin is released from prison to live out his life in Babylon. 2 Kings 25:27-30, Jeremiah 52:31-34 Neriglissar (Nergal-sharizer) son-in-law of Nebuchadnezzar assassinated Amel-Marduk and reigneed from 560 to 556.

556 B.C. Reign of Labas-Marduk son of Neriglissar.

556 B.C. Reign of Nabonidus (556-539). From 553-544 he reigned from Tema in Arabia. He returned to Babylon in 544 B.C.

553 B.C. Beginning of the co-regency of Belshazzar (553-539) son of Nabonidus and grandson of Nebuchadnezzar. His mother was a daughter of Nebuchadnezzar.

539 B.C. Babylon falls to the Medes and Persians.

539 B.C. Cyrus (539-530) becomes ruler of the Medio-Persian Empire. Daniel is still serving in the king's court. (Daniel 1:21) Cyrus issued his edict that the Jews may return to Jerusalem to rebuild the temple.

536 B.C. Last historical reference to Daniel (Daniel 10: 1)

530 B.C. Beginning of the reign of Cambyses (530-522)

522 B.C. Beginning of the reign of Darius I (522-486) (Haggai 1:1, Zechariah 4:5)

486 B.C. Beginning of the reign of Xerxes (Ahasuerus of Esther) (486-470)

A Snapshot of Hosea

Author

Unstated in text.

Date of Ministry and Writing

Hosea ministered between 790 and 685 B.C. [1:1]. He most likely began his ministry in the last days of Jeroboam 2 @ 782-753 B.C. The book was probably written @ 715 B.C.

Recipients

The northern kingdom of Israel, as seen in the many references to Ephraim (as leader of the Northern Tribes)

Theme

In spite of Israel's unfaithfulness, Yahweh's faithful love will prevail to purify and restore Israel for Himself.

Purpose

To encourage repentance. To explain to the righteous why judgment is coming and to assure them of restoration.

The Story

What is unique about Hosea's story is how God used

Hosea's personal life as a prophetic message to Israel. First God told Hosea to marry an immoral woman and have children. [1:2]S o, Hosea married Gomer the daughter of Diblaim.

Gomer gave birth to two sons and a daughter though it is not clear from the text whether they were actually Hosea's [2:4]. Because of her unfaithfulness Hosea divorced her and sent her away. [2:2]

She evidently fell into a deplorable state and only survived by the secret provision Hosea provided for her [2:8] In 3:1-3 God commanded Hosea to take her back. So, he bought her out of a slave market and commanded her to be a faithful wife. We know nothing more about his life.

Outline

1. Hosea Displays the Message 1-3

  1) First life message 1:2-2:1

  2) Message application 2:2-2:23

  3) Second life message 3:1-5

2. Hosea Declares the Message 4-14

  1) The covenant lawsuit 4:1-3

2) First complaint: no knowledge of God 4:4—6:3

3) Second complaint: no loyalty 6:4-11:11

4) Third complaint: no reliability 11:12-14:9

Characteristics and Points of Interest:

1. Hosea was a contemporary of Isaiah and Micah.
2. Hosea is one of the prophets (along with Isaiah) whose life was used as a message to God's people.
3. The story about Hosea's wife Gomer has been variously interpreted.

    1) God did not actually tell Hosea to literally do this, this was only symbolic. There was no real Gomer.

    2) Gomer was not a literal harlot, but only a member of a nation that was a harlot nation.

    3) Gomer only became a harlot after she married Hosea. She is described in 1:2 in terms of what she would later become.

4) God told Hosea to marry an immoral woman. She also committed adultery after he married her. Did she remain faithful after 3:3? Why would God command Hosea to marry an immoral woman (or a women God knew would become

170

unfaithful)? Hosea's life is going to be a prophetic message.

4.The man and his story: God commanded Hosea to marry Gomer, an immoral woman (1:2). He married her and fathered a son (1:2). She had 2 other children (whether they are Hosea's or not the text doesn't say (1:6,8). Hosea put her out (2:2). God commanded him to take her again (3:1). So, he bought her out of a slave market (3:2) and commanded her to be faithful (3:3).

5. The price for which Hosea bought Gomer was half the price of a common slave. Barley which was grain usually fed to livestock.

6. Each of the complaints of chapters 4-14 contains 3 parts:

A statement of condemnation 4:4-5:7, 6:4-7:16, 11:12-12:14

A decree of punishment 5:8-15, 8:1-10:15, 13:1-16

A promise of restoration 6:1-3, 11:1-11, 14:1-9

7. 4:1-3 is a formal legal case, the indictment.

Major Applications

1. The ever-active love of God to restore the fallen, to bring us back to himself.
2. The tragedy of sin, what it brings about in our lives.
3. The sinfulness of sin. The depravity of the human heart in spurning God's love.
4. The shamefulness of sin. The shame it brings to us and the pain it brings to God and others.
5. The necessity of internalizing spiritual truth. External worship without internal reality is worthless and vain.
6. A call to repentance.

Recommended Resources

J. Andrew Dearman, The Book of Hosea, [NICOT] Eerdmans, 2010

Charles Feinberg, The Minor Prophets, Moody Press, 1951

John Goldingay, Hosea-Micah, Baker, 2021

*G. C. Morgan, Hosea: The Heart and Holiness of God, Baker, 1999

A Snapshot of Joel

Author

The Joel, son of Pethuel 1:1. The prophecies were given by Joel we do not know who compiled them in this book. We know nothing more about Joel.

Date of Ministry

The prophecies and their composition @ 841-796 B.C.

1. After good King Jehoshaphat [848 B.C.] but before the rise of the Great kingdoms of Assyria and Babylon. The enemies listed in Joel are Egypt, Tyre and Sidon (Phoenicia), and the Philistine cities [3:4. 19)]

2. Since locusts and drought were evidences of the judgment of God (e.g. Deuteronomy 28:3 8), Joel's ministry was during a time of disobedience.

   1) Perhaps during the reign of Ahaziah or Athaliah

   2) Or during the later part of Joash' s reign, after the death of Jehoiada. 2 Chronicles 24:2, 18, 19) @ 800 B.C.

3) Perhaps during the early years of Joash @ 830, because no king is mentioned as the prophets usually do, because Jehoiada was the virtual ruler.

4) Another argument for this early date of Joel is the apparent quotes of Joel.

Joel 3:16 is quoted in Amos 1:2 and Joel 1:15 in Isaiah 13:6

Recipients

The Southern Kingdom of Judah. Note the references to Judah and Jerusalem. 2:15, 23, 32; 3:18, 20)

Theme

A warning of divine judgment in the Day of the Lord.

Purpose

To warn Judah of coming judgment to turn them back to God.

The Story

A current locust plague and drought is the impetus for these prophecies of future events.

Outline

1. The Day of the Lord Pictured 1:1-20

    1) The present judgment of locusts v.1-12

    2) The present judgment of drought v.13-20

  2. The Day of the Lord Prophesied 2:1-3:21

    1) Judgment proclaimed 2:1-11

2) Repentance and prayer urged 2:12-17

3) Restoration of Israel revealed 2:18-32

4) Judgment on the nations asserted 3:1-17

5) Millennial blessings announced 3:18-21

Characteristics and Points of Interest

1. The day of the Lord refers to the Tribulation, Second Coming and Millennial Reign of Christ, both judgment and blessing are included.

2. Joel 2:28-32 is a separate chapter in the Hebrew Old Testament.

3. Joel 2:28-32 is not being fulfilled in today's charismatic movement. Joel 2:28-32 is concerned with Israel and is a millennial promise. Joel 2 looks primarily to the future (end times), but it speaks of it in terms of the present judgment of the locusts. The "after this" of v. 28 goes back to v. 20 — the destruction of the northern army, of Israel's enemies. So the events of v. 28 will take place after the tribulational judgments.

The millennial outpouring of the Spirit is a repeated Old Testament promise.

Jeremiah 31:31-ff, Isaiah 32:15, Ezekiel 36:27-28, 37:14,

39:29, Zechariah 12:10. The deliverance of v. 32 is from death in the tribulational judgments and entrance into the millennium. V. 23 The "early rains" refer to the Davidic Kingdom, The "latter rains" to the Messianic Kingdom. What is the meaning of Peter's quotation of Joel 2:28-32 in Acts 2:14-21? Peter does not say the Pentecost experience totally fulfilled this text. Verses 19-20 were not fulfilled at all. Then what does Peter mean?

1) That the pouring out of the Spirit at Pentecost was an illustration of what

would happen in The End Times.

2) The pouring-out of the Spirit upon the remnant (believing Jews) at Pentecost was a sign that the Kingdom was at hand. Indeed, it could have come if the Jews had repented (Acts 3:19-26). With their rejection the final fulfillment of the passage must await the return of Christ. What began to happen at Pentecost will be completed when Christ returns.

4. Joel uses a current crisis [a locust plague] as the framework for forecasting the future. Bible teachers debate whether 2:2-11 is a reference to the current locust plague or a metaphorical description of end time events.

Major Applications

1. For warning believers as to the consequences of sin.

2. For encouragement of forgiveness and blessings which follow repentance.

3. For understanding of the events related to Christ's second coming.

4. For understanding that God can chasten sin through natural disasters.

Recommended Resources

Leslie Allen, The Books of Joel, Obadiah, Jonah and Micah, [NICOT] Eerdmans, 1976

Charles Feinberg, The Minor Prophets, Moody Press, 1976

Duane A. Garrett and Paul Ferris, Hosea, Joel, Holman, 1997

*David Levy, Joel: The Day of the Lord, Friends of Israel, 1987

Walter K. Price, The Prophet Joel and the Day of the Lord, Moody Press, 1976

A Snapshot of Amos

Author

These were the prophecies of Amos, a shepherd from Tekoa 1:1 We don't know who compiled them. The vision of chapters 7-9 are direct reports from Amos.

Date of Ministry and Writing

During the reigns of King Uzziah of Judah [790-739 B.C.)]and Jeroboam II of Israel [793-753 B.C.]. As Uzziah was a coregent until 767 B.C. it seems best to place Amos' ministry between [767-753 B.C.] and the date of writing @ 760-750 B.C.

Recipients

Amos' primary ministry seems to have been in and to Israel (northern kingdom) [1:1, 7:10-17, 9:1,3:9,12, 4:1]. However, some of his words are directed to and about Judah [6:1, 14, 2:4-5]. So, perhaps, it is best to suggest that the book was intended for both Israel and Judah, though especially for Israel.

Theme

God's righteous judgment on Israel and the nations accords with His covenant promises.

Purpose

To warn Israel of impending judgment so as to bring about repentance.

The Story

We know little about Amos' story. He was a shepherd and farmer from Tekoa who saw these prophetic visions. The only historical incident the book records is when Amaziah a priest in Bethel complained to King Jeroboam II about Amos. Amaziah told Amos to flee to Judah. [7:10-17]

Outline

1. General proclamation of judgment 1:3-2:16

   1) Against the nations 1:3-2:3 Damascus (Syria) 1:3-5, Gaza (Philistia) 1:6-8, Tyre 1:9-10, Edom 1: 11-12, Ammon 1:13-15, and Moab 2:1-3

   2) Against Judah 2:4-5

   3) Against Israel 2:6-16 (1) Accusation 6-12, (2) Judgment 13-16

2. Proclamation of judgment against Israel. 3:1-6:14

1) First message: The basis of judgment 3:1-15

(1) Divine basis v. 1-2

(2) Logical basis v. 3-8

(3) Call for witnesses v. 9-10

(4) Pronouncement of judgment. v. 11-15

2) Second message: The cause for judgment 4:1-13

(1) They had committed social and religious sins v. 1-5

(2) They had not heeded God's warnings v. 6-13: famine (v1-6), drought (v.7-8), pestilence (v.9), plagues and military defeat (v.10) overthrow (v. 11), and conclusion (v.12-13)

3) Third message: A dirge for Israel 5:1-6:14

(1) The lament 5:1-3

(2) An appeal to repent 5:4-15 The appeal given v. 4-9, rejected v. 10-13 and renewed v. 14-15

4) A prophecy of the captivity: (1) cause: corruption 5:16-6:6, (2) the consequences: judgment 6:7-14 [exile]

3. Five visions of judgment 7:1-9:15

1) Locust swarm 7:1-3

2) Fire 7:4-6

3) Plumb line 7:7-9

4) Historical interlude: Rejection of the message 7:10-17

5) Fruit Basket 8:1-14

6) The Lord beside the altar 9:1-15

Characteristics and Points of Interest

1. Each of the three messages of chapters 3-6 is introduced with the appeal "Hear this Word". The first message deals with the present (3). The second looks to the past (4). The third looks to the future (5-6).

2. At the time of Amos' ministry Israel was strong and secure politically. Economically there was unprecedented wealth for a rich minority and abject poverty for the vast majority. Socially, morally and spiritually it was a time of decadence and corruption. (greed 6:4-6, injustice 4: 1, 5:10-12, 3 8, immorality 3:7, 8, idolatry 2:8, 5:5, 25-26, and empty ritualism 2:8, 4:4-5, 5:21-24)

3. The expression "for three transgressions and four" means "one too many, past the point of no return" [1:3,6,9,11,13,2:1,4,6]

4. The cows of 4:1 are wealthy women.

5. Each of the visions of 7-9 has its own focus.

Locusts/fire-God's longsuffering "withheld"

Plumb line -They didn't measure up. Their land will be parceled up.

181

Summer fruit -Judgment is imminent.

The Lord by the altar -Judgment is not final. Remnant and restoration.

6. Amos like many other prophets of God found that his ministry was rejected. 7:10-13

7. Only Amos, Jonah, and Hosea are particularly directed to Israel. (north)

8. Amos was perhaps contemporary with Jonah and Hosea

Major Applications

1.Amos is a call to repentance.

2. Rejecting the Word of the Lord is the cause of the judgment of God. (2:4)

3. God cares about social justice and moral uprightness in a society. Injustice and immorality will bring a country to ruin.

4. Sin against others is sin against God.

5. The foolishness and wickedness of failure to heed the warnings of God.

6. The longsuffering of God in seeking to restore us through warnings and pleas.

7. God will not accept hypocritical worship. (4:4—5)

8. God's gracious election brings us great responsibility. (3:1—2)

9.Religion will not tolerate the truth. Those who reject God's message will often reject God's messengers and accuse them of improper motives.

10.Amos like, other prophets was rejected. Success in ministry is not always the mark of God's favor or failure God's disfavor.

Recommended Resources

T. J. Betts, <u>Amos: An Ordinary Man with an Extraordinary Focus,</u> Christian Focus, 2011

Charles Feinberg, <u>The Minor Prophets</u>, Moody Press, 1976

*JoAnna Hoyt and H Wayne House, <u>Amos, Jonah and Micah: An Evangelical Exegetical   Commentary,</u> Lexham, 2019

A Snapshot of Obadiah

Author

Obadiah received the visions. He may have compiled them.

Date of Writing

Shortly after the fall of Jerusalem. Edom's participation or encouragement of the destruction of Jerusalem. [Psalms 137:7, Lamentations 4:21, 22, Ezekiel 25:12-14, 35:5ff, Jeremiah 49:7-22, Amos 1:11, 12].

Recipients

The Jewish exiles

Theme

God will bring judgment upon Edom.

Purpose

To assure the remnant that God has not forgotten their plight and those who rejoiced in their downfall and to demonstrate that God has not been defeated by the gods of the pagans.

The Story

These prophecies are the response of Obadiah to the compliance of the Edomites in the destruction of Jerusalem by the Babylonians in 586 B.C.

Outline

1. The Revelation of Edom's coming destruction. v. 1-9

2. The Reason for Edom's coming destruction. v. 10-14

3. The Results of the Day of the Lord. v. 15-21

   1) Retribution on the Nations. v. 15-16

   2) Restitution of Judah. v. 17-21

Characteristics and Points of Interest

1. The Edomites were descendants from Esau who lived in an area stretching from Wadi Zered at the southeastern tip of the Dead Sea to the Gulf of Aqabah and both sides of the Arabah. Their enmity against Israel is foretold in Genesis 27.
2. Edom had refused the Israelites passage across their land toward Canaan. Numbers 20:14-21 The Land of Edom was not included in the Promised Land. Later, Edom had conflict with Saul and was conquered and subjugated by David and Solomon. Edom revolted. After the fall of Jerusalem, they invaded the heart of southern Judah.
3. The fulfillment of this prophecy began with subjugation by the Babylonians. In 312 B.C. the Arabians forced them to flee to Idumaea (southern Judah) John Hyrcanus, a Jewish

patriot, subdued them in 126 B.C. and compelled them to be circumcised. The Romans completed their destruction.

4. Herod the Great was a man of Jewish and Edomite descent.

5. Obadiah was contemporary with Jeremiah, Daniel and Ezekiel.

Major Applications

1. God keeps his word. The Abrahamic Covenant of blessing and cursing is behind Edom's destruction. Genesis 12:3

2. God does not condone sin, even though he may use sinners and their sin as a means of executing his will.

3. The danger of pride. The best military defense (Petra) possible to men will not save a country God desires to bring down

Recommended Resources

*Leslie Allen, The Books of Joel, Obadiah, Jonah and Micah, [NICOT] Eerdmans, 1976

Daniel L. Block, Obadiah: A Discussion Analysis, [ECOT] Zondervan, 2017

Charles Feinberg, The Minor Prophets, Moody Press, 1976

A Snapshot of Jonah

Author

Unstated but probably Jonah the Son of Amitti. Jonah is mentioned also in 2 Kings 14:25 which says that Jonah was from Gath-hepher (in Zebulun).

Date of Ministry

@ 780-760 B.C. during the reign of Jeroboam II of Israel.

Recipients

Though the prophetic ministry of Jonah recorded in Jonah was to Nineveh, the capitol of Assyria, the book was intended for the people of Israel.

Theme

God's mercy and compassion extend even to Gentile nations who repent.

Purpose

1.To bring about repentance in a time when Israel was no better than the Gentiles morally and spiritually.

2. To show that God may accomplish his work even through disobedient servants.

3.To teach the righteous but prideful, remnant compassion.

No matter how wicked the wicked may be God will forgive the repentant

4. To teach Israel that what is important is not nationality, but righteousness.

5. God used a plant and a worm to teach Jonah a lesson about compassion.

The Story

God called Jonah to go to Nineveh, the capital of Assyria to proclaim its coming destruction. Jonah did not want to go and attempted to flee to Tarshish (an opposite direction from Nineveh. God sent a storm of the Mediterranean which was only quelled when Jonah was thrown overboard. God provided a great fish to swallow Jonah. There in the fish for three days Jonah prayed, and God caused the fish to vomit Jonah on dry land. A second time God told Jonah to go to Nineveh. This time he went, and the city of Nineveh responded to his message by repenting, causing God to turn away from his intentions to destroy the city. This greatly angered Jonah who waited outside the city to see its destruction.

Outline

1. Jonah Runs from God 1

2. Jonah Runs to God 2

3. Jonah Runs for God 3

4. Jonah Resents God 4

Characteristics and Points of Interest

1. Jonah was contemporary with the prophet Amos.

2. Jonah's sea experience is cited as a type of Christ's death and resurrection. in Matthew 12:38-41.

3. The Bible does not identify Jonah's host as a whale, rather a "great fish". Whales and some sharks have this capacity.

4. Nineveh was a royal city of Assyria, an expanding world power known for its cruel atrocities.

5. The three-day journey (3:3) probably refers to the circumference of the greater administrative district rather than the city proper.

6. The 120,000 (4:11) "who do not know the difference between right and left hand" probably refers to young children. So, the population of Nineveh was probably around 600,000.

7. Some suggest that Jonah's life as recorded here is a prophecy of the future of the nation of Israel.

8. At the time of Jonah's ministry Israel had one of her most powerful kings on the throne and the surrounding Gentile states were relatively weak.

9. Grace is displayed in every chapter of the book.1:15,17,2:10, 3:1,10, 4:6,11

Major Applications

1.To convince people of God's impartial mercy. He seeks and saves the lost, whoever they may be, however wicked they may be.

2.To show us the sinfulness of pride, rebellion, and hatred.

3. To demonstrate God's work in the lives of those whom He would use to serve Him to accomplish His purposes.

Recommended Resources

Leslie Allen, The Books of Joel, Obadiah, Jonah and Micah, [NICOT] Eerdmans, 1976

JoAnna Hoyt and H Wayne House, Amos, Jonah and Micah: An Evangelical Exegetical   Commentary, Lexham, 2019

Thomas E. McComiskey The Minor Prophets: A Commentary on Obadiah, Jonah, Micah, Nahum, and Habakkuk, Baker , 2018

*Daniel Timmer, A Gracious and Compassionate God, IVP, 2018

A Snapshot of Micah

Author

Micah of Moresheth (A village in the lowlands of Judah)

Date of Ministry and Writing

Micah's ministry was during the reigns of the Judean kings: Jotham, Ahaz, and Hezekiah [750-686 B.C.] Chapter 1 is before 722 B.C. as Samaria had not yet been destroyed. No other time indications given directly in the book. The book was written @ 700 B.C. Jeremiah 26:18 identifies the prophecy of Micah 3:12 as coming during the reign of Hezekiah.

Recipients

Judah, primarily, but his ministry was not exclusively to Judah (south) Chapter 1 is primarily a message against Israel) (north)

Theme:

The necessary product of delivering faith is social reform and practical holiness.

Purpose

1. To show to Judah the necessity of social justice and

practical holiness in order to avert judgment and bring about repentance

2. to assure the righteous remnant of restoration.

Outline

Prologue 1:1

1. The judgment and restoration of Israel and Judah. 1:2-2:13

    1) The judgment of Israel announced 1:2-7

    2) The lament of the prophet. 1:**8**

    3) The judgment of Judah 1:9-16

    4) The cause of the judgment. 2:1-2

    5) The consequences of sin. 2:3-5

    6) Contention of people with the prophet 2:6-11

    7) Consolation 2: 12-13

2. The judgment and restoration of Judah 3:1-4:13

    1) Condemnation 3:1-12

        (1) Condemnation of rulers 3:1-4

        (2) Condemnation of religious leaders 3:5-8

        (3) Condemnation of Jerusalem's rulers 3: 12

2) Future restoration 4:1-8

    (1) Restoration of Jerusalem and the temple 4:1-2

    (2) Peace and prosperity under God's judge 4:3-4

    (3) Response of the Righteous. 4:5

    (4) Return of the exiles and God's rule 4:6-8

3) The exile in Babylon and return 4:9-10

4) Victory over the enemy nations. 4:11-13

5) The present devastation. 5:1

6) The birth and deliverance of God's Ruler. 5:2-6

7) The victory and purification of the remnant 5:7-14

    (1) Victory 5:7-9 (2) Purification 5:10-14

  8) The judgment of the nations. 5:15

3. The covenant lawsuit against Judah. 6:1-7:20

1) The lawsuit 6:1-16

2) The prophet's response 7:1-14

3) Yahweh's answer 7:15

4) Climatic prophecy and praise 7: 16-17

5) Praise for God's Faithfulness. 7:18-20

Characteristics and Points of Interest

1. Micah was a contemporary of Isaiah and Hosea. See Isaiah 1:1 and Hosea 1:1

2. Micah is quoted 3 times in the Bible:
    1) Micah 4:12. By the elders of Judah in Jeremiah 26: 18
    2) Micah 5:2. By the Chief Priest and Scribes in Matthew 2:5- Micah 7:6, and (3) By Jesus in Matthew. 10:35-36

3. Micah 4:1-3 and Isaiah 2:2-4 are nearly identical.

4. Jewish worshippers read the closing verses of Micah 7: 18-20 on the Day of Atonement.

5. Chapter 6 consists of a formal covenant lawsuit against Judah. It follows the form of such ancient lawsuits: Call together of witnesses v. 1-2, a recital of the benevolent acts of the sovereign v. 3-5, introductory statement of the charge v. 6-8, the indictment proper v. 9-12, and the sentence v. 13-16 Other such prophetic lawsuits are found in Hosea 4 and Jeremiah 2.

6. Among the predictions of Micah are:

The fall of Samaria [1:6], the invasion of Judah by Assyria [1:9-16], the destruction of Jerusalem [3:12], exile of Judah in Babylon [4:10], the Millennial reign of the Messiah]4:1-

8], and birth of the Messianic King in Bethlehem [5:2].

7. It would appear that the preaching of Isaiah and Micah were instrumental to the reforms of Hezekiah.

8. The major divisions of the book are marked by the prophet's call to "Hear" the message. 1 :2,

9. Micah 6:8 is a concise summary of the message of Micah to the people.

10. Micah's response to the messages are found in 1:8, 3:1, 8, 4:5, 6:6, and 7:7

Major Applications

1. God is faithful to His Word. He will do as He has spoken whether in judgment or restoration,

2. Spiritual reality is demonstrated by and must be accompanied by social justice and moral holiness.

3. We must walk humbly and obediently before the Lord. Externalism and religious formalism are not good enough.

4. Hope of salvation rests in God's love and forgiveness.

Recommended Resources

Leslie Allen, The Books of Joel, Obadiah, Jonah and Micah, [NICOT] Eerdmans, 1976

Charles Feinberg, The Minor Prophets, Moody Press, 1976

Thomas E. McComiskey The Minor Prophets: A Commentary on Obadiah, Jonah, Micah, Nahum, and Habakkuk, Baker, 2018

*Bruce K. Waltke, A Commentary on Micah, Eerdmans, 2007

A Snapshot of Nahum

Author

Nahum. The messages are Nahum's. Compiler is unknown

Date of Writing and Events

Sometime during the reign of Ashurbanipal of Assyria [669-627 B.C.], during the reign of Josiah of Judah [640-609 B.C.] before the fall of Nineveh in 612 B.C.

Recipients

Though the words are directed, for the most part, to Nineveh (Assyria), the ultimate recipients of the book were God's people in Judah. Some texts directly address Judah. [1:7-8, 12b-13, 15, 2:2]

Theme

Wicked Nineveh (Assyria) will fall before the mighty and holy God of Judah.

Purpose

To encourage the embattled people of Judah during the reign of the king Josiah.

Outline

1. Judgment of Nineveh declared 1

   1) Basis: the character of God v. 2-8

   2) Evil plans judged v. 9-15

2. Judgment of Nineveh described 2

   1) Call to Nineveh v. 1-2

   2) Destruction visualized v. 3-10

   3) The Lord's pronouncement of judgment v. 11-13

3. Judgment of Nineveh defended 3

   1) By the evilness of the city v. 1-7

   2) By the example of No-Amen v. 8-13

   3) By their inability to overcome it v. 14-19

Characteristics and Points of Interest

1, Historically the destruction of Nineveh took place in 612 B.C. at the hands of Babylonians, Medes and Scythians.

2.The historical record shows that the seemingly impregnable city walls were breached due to a Tigris River flood that weakened the walls. [1:8]

3. Nineveh became a grave [1:14]. The site of Nineveh was not clearly identified until 1845 AD.

199

4. Nahum was the second Hebrew prophet to address Nineveh. (The first was Jonah 130 to 140 years earlier.)

5. Nineveh was the capital city of the greatest world power of that time, Assyria. It was strongly fortified [3:12]. So sure were the Assyrians of their defenses that the king and Assyrian army were given over to excessive drinking and partying.

6. Nahum 3:7, 19 is understandable considering the Assyrian's reputation for delighting in immorality and cruelty in war. They were known for piling the heads of enemies as monuments of victory, boiling enemies in oil, tearing off arms and legs, skinning people alive, pulling out tongues and impaling them on stakes.

7. The curses of Nahum closely parallel curses found in the vassal treaties imposed on subjugated kings by the Assyrian kings Esarhaddon (681-669 B.C.) and his son Ashurbanipal (669-627 B.C.). This parallel is probably intentional. Nahum invokes twelve commonly used curses, typical of the Assyrian treaties against the Assyrians themselves. This also serves as a polemic against false gods of Assyria, whom the Assyrians credited for their military victories.

8. The disposition of the prophet: he is emotionally stirred up about this message, resorting to many figures of speech,

sarcasm and irony.

10. Note: fulfilled prophecies of 1:10,14, 2:6

11. Nahum l:15 is quoted in Romans 10:15 as being typical of those who proclaim The Gospel.

12. One of the most comforting verses of the Old Testament is found in Nahum 1:7.

13. The "one" mentioned in 1:11 is Sennacherib who invaded Judah in 701 B.C. when Hezekiah was the king of Judah.

14. Nahum was contemporary with Zephaniah and Jeremiah and perhaps Habakkuk.

Major Applications

1. God is still on the throne. The mightiest of world powers cannot stand if God determines otherwise. 1-9
2. God is against the wicked 1:2. There is hope in him for the righteous. 1:7
3. Kingdoms built by violence and wickedness will perish the same way. God is just. God's punishment fits the crime.

Recommended Resources

Charles L. Feinberg, The Minor Prophets, Moody, 1976

*Eric C. Redmond, Exalting Jesus in Jonah, Micah, Nahum and Habakkuk, Holman, 2016

O Palmer Robertson, The Books of Nahum, Habakkuk, and Zephaniah, [NICOT] Eerdmans, 2021

Daniel Timmer and Daniel Block, Nahum: Discourse and Analysis, Zondervan, 2019

A Snapshot of Habakkuk

Author

Habakkuk. Compiler unknown

Date of Ministry and Writing

Evidently during the years after the reign of the good King Josiah and before the end of the kingdom of Judah. So, between 609-586 B.C.)

Recipients

The Jews either before or during the exile.

Theme

The coming judgment of Judah through the Babylonians is righteous (justifiable) and deserved. But the just will live by faith in the face of apparent hindrances to God's prophetic promises.

Purpose

To explain the coming judgment to the righteous remnant. To encourage trust in the Lord despite the terrible coming disaster.

The Story

The book of Habakkuk records a conversation between God and Habakkuk. The story begins with Haggai's complaint that the Lord was not doing anything about the sin of the people and his shock that God would use the wicked Babylonians to punish his people.

The story ends with his statement of joy in the Lord in spite of his circumstances.

Outline

1. The question about Judah's sins. 1:1-11

    1) The prophet's question about sin v.2-4

    2) God's answer: The Chaldeans are coming to judge v.5-11

2. The question about judgment 1:12-2:20

    1) The Prophet's question about judgment [1:12-2:1]

    2) God's answer [2:2-20)] The Babylonians will be destroyed.

    3) A message to the righteous 2:4, 5

    4) Five woes upon the Chaldeans 2:6-20

3. The supplication by the prophet 3: 1-19a

    1) The prophet's petition v. 1-2

2) A vision of God's coming in judgment and in

   deliverance v.3-15

3) The prophet's response v. 16-19

Characteristics and Points of Interest

1. Chapters 1 and 2 are prose. Chapter 3 is poetic hymn.
3:19.

2. The attitudes of the prophet are crucial to understanding this book. 1:1-11-impatient, 1:12-17-indignant/shocked, 2:1-arrogant, 3:1-16-fearful, 3:17-19 -trusting.

3. The proud one of 2:4 refers to either the Chaldeans or the prophet.

4. The immediate meaning of the often-quoted phrase of 2:4 "The just shall live by his faith" seems to be that the righteous remnant will survive the Chaldean onslaught by their continuing faithfulness to God's law and worship. But since faithfulness is the result of faith (and the Hebrew word can mean either) the Apostle Paul is quite justified in his application of the idea to salvation. [Romans 1:17, Galatians 3:11]. The phrase "shall live" means "shall have life" rather than "shall live his life by."

Major Applications

1. We must never forget that God is just and righteous in his dealings. Don't become impatient with the Lord. Joshua 5:7, 8

2. A call to trust the Lord in difficult times. This call to faith is also a call to faithfulness.

Recommended Resources

Charles L. Feinberg, The Minor Prophets, Moody, 1976

Thomas E. McComiskey, The Minor Prophets: A Commentary on Obadiah, Jonah, Micah, Nahum, Habakkuk Baker, 2018

*Eric C. Redmond, Exalting Jesus in in Jonah, Micah, Nahum and Habakkuk, Holman, 2016

O Palmer Robertson, The Books of Nahum, Habakkuk and Zephaniah, [NICOT] Eerdmans, 2021

A Snapshot of Zephaniah

Author

Zephaniah [1:1]

Date of Ministry and Writing

Zephaniah ministered during the reign of Josiah [640-609 B.C]. His ministry seems to have been before Josiah's reform [628 B.C.] and was perhaps part of the reason for that reform. The book was written about the same time, so between 640-628 B.C.

Recipients

Judah

Theme

The Day of the Lord is coming. He will punish the disobedient and save the righteous remnant.

Purpose

To bring about repentance.

Outline

1. The judgment of the Day of the Lord **1:1-3:7**

    1) Upon Judah 1:1-2:3

        (1) Near prophecy 1:2-13

        (2) Far prophecy 1:14-18

        (3) Appeal to repent 2:1-3

    2) Upon the nations 2:4-15

        (1) Philistia 2:4-7 (west)

        (2) Moab 2:8-11 (east)

        (3) Ethiopia 2:12 (south)

        (4) Assyria 2:13-15 (north)

    3) Upon Jerusalem 3:1-7

2. The salvation of the Day of the Lord 3:8-20

    1) The purging of the remnant 3:8-13

    2) The joy of the Lord's presence 3:14-20

Characteristics and Points of Interest

1.   There are three significant events in Josiah's reign. 2 Chronicles 34—35 1) 632 B.C. He began to seek the Lord.

1)   628 B.C.   He began to purge Judah of idolatry.

2)   622 B.C.   The book of the law was found and lawful worship was reestablished.

2. In spite of Josiah's reforms, the doom of Judah was already set. [2 Kings 22:18-20]

3. Zephaniah was a contemporary with Nahum and Jeremiah.

4. The Day of the Lord is not only a future event, finding its ultimate fulfillment in the end times, it is also a situation always true and repeatable.

5. Zephaniah's theme, the Day of the Lord, is also the theme of Joel.

6. Zephaniah may have been of royalty if Hezekiah (1:1) refers to King Hezekiah.

Major Applications

1. God always deals with us in accordance with His eternal character and purposes. He is the same God now as He was in the time of Zephaniah. This brings us warning and assurance.

2. The relationship between the prophets and the reforms or revivals gives us encouragement in serving Christ.

Recommended Resources

Charles L. Feinberg, <u>The Minor Prophets</u>, Moody, 1976

Thomas E. McComiskey, <u>The Minor Prophets: A Commentary on Zephaniah, Haggai, Zechariah, and Malachi,</u> Baker, 2018

*O Palmer Robertson, <u>The Books of Nahum, Habakkuk and Zephaniah,</u> [NICOT] Eerdmans, 2021

S. D. Snyman, <u>s</u>, IVP, 2020

A Snapshot of Haggai

Author

Haggai

Date of Events

@ 519 B.C. In 538 B.C. the remnant returned to rebuild the temple at Jerusalem [Ezra 1:1]. But after the altar of burnt offering and the foundation were completed the work stopped. [Ezra 3:2, 11] Date of Writing: @ 519 B.C.

Recipients

The remnant of returned Jewish exiles.

Theme

Seek God and His work, and He will bring blessing.

Purpose

To exhort the remnant to complete the task of rebuilding the temple.

The Story

Haggai and Zechariah were the two prophets whose encouragement spurred the returned remnant to resume building the temple in Jerusalem. [Ezra 4:24-5:2, 6:14]

Outline

1. A Word of reproof [1:2-15]

2. A Word of support [2:1-9]

3. A Word of blessing [2:10-19]

4. A Word of promise [2:20-23]

Characteristics and Points of Interest

1. These messages give us the gist of Haggai's preaching, which along with preaching of Zechariah motivated the people to return to the task of rebuilding the temple. Haggai 1 Ezra 5:1-2

2. The support of Haggai and Zechariah was crucial to this task. Ezra 5:2, 6:14

Major Applications

1. The importance of putting God and His work first in our lives.

2. The importance of encouraging and exhorting each other.

3. The encouragement value of the promises of God.

4. How to overcome discouragement.

5. The principles of cause and effect.

6. The importance of keeping an eternal perspective.

Recommended Resources

Charles L. Feinberg, The Minor Prophets, Moody, 1976

John L. Mackay, Haggai, Zechariah, and Malachi: God's Restored People, Christian Focus 2010

Thomas E. McComiskey, The Minor Prophets: A Commentary on Zephaniah, Haggai, Zechariah, and Malachi, Baker, 2018

Eugene H. Merrill, Haggai, Zechariah, and Malachi: An Exegetical Commentary, Create Space, 2014

*Peter Verhoef, The books of Haggai and Malachi, [NICOT] Eerdmans, 1987

Snapshot of Zechariah

Author

Zechariah. The visions of chapters 1-7 are first person accounts of what Zechariah saw and heard. Compiler is unknown.

Date of Events

From 520 to 470 B.C.

Date of Writing

@ 470 B.C.

Recipients

The returned remnant of the Jews from exile in Babylon

Theme

God is going to preserve His remnant from all the world powers. He rules through His Word.

Purpose

To give the returned remnant confidence in the Word of God in the times of Gentile dominion.

The Story

Zechariah [along with Haggai] was one of the prophets who spurred the returned remnant to resume the work on the temple. [Ezra 4:24-5:2, 6:14] We know nothing more about him

Outline

1. Historical prologue 1:1-6

2. The Word of the Lord in visions 1:7-6:15

    1) The rider on the red horse 1:7-17 — need for judgment

    2) The four horsemen and four craftsmen 1:18-21 —the

        agents of judgment

    3) The man with the measuring line 2:1-13 — the

        restoration of Jerusalem

    4) Joshua and Satan 3:1-10 — the cleansing of the nation

    5) The lampstand and olive trees 4:1-14 — a witness to

        the nation is established

    6) The flying scroll 5:1-4—the curse of the law

    7) The ephah and the woman 5:6-11 — the removal of

215

commercial sin

8) The four chariots 6: 1-8—the judgments of the

Tribulation

9) The historical crowning of the King/Priest 6:9-15 —

the millennial reign of the Messiah

3. The Word of the Lord in dialogue. 7:1-8:23

1) The negative word -accusation of insincerity and

hardness 7:1-14

2) The positive word -the Lord's love and purpose for Zion

8:1-23

4. The Word of God in oracle. 9:1-14:21

1) The overthrow of the nations. 9:1-11:17

2) The purification of Israel 12:1-14:21

Characteristics and Points of Interest:

1. What Revelation is to the New Testament Zechariah is to
the Old Testament. (Summation of prophetic revelation)
12. Haggai and Zechariah were the prophets who inspired
the people to complete the rebuilding of the temple. [Ezra 5:
1-2, 6: 1]4

3. Chapters 1-8 are primarily historical, with extensions relating to the end times. Chapters 9-14 are primarily futuristic.

4. The key theme of Zechariah is the Word of the Lord.

5. Zechariah includes several important prophecies. Christ as the King/ Priest 6:9-15, the triumphant entry 9:9, the piercing of the Messiah 12:10, and the second coming of Christ onto the Mt. of Olives 14:4

6. Zechariah is filled with promises.

Major Applications

1. God's Word — By His Word He will accomplish His Work.

2. Assurance that God's plan will be fulfilled.

3. The centrality of Christ.

4. The importance of knowing the promises of God for motivation.

Recommended Resources

Mark Boda, The Book of Zechariah, [NICOT], Eerdmans, 2016

Charles L Feinberg, The Minor Prophets, Moody, 1976

George Klein, Zechariah, Holman, 2016

John L. Mackay, Haggai, Zechariah, and Malachi: God's Restored People, Christian Focus , 2010

Thomas E. McComiskey, The Minor Prophets: A Commentary on Zephaniah, Haggai, Zechariah, and Malachi, Baker, 2018

Eugene H. Merrill, Haggai, Zechariah, and Malachi: An Exegetical Commentary, Create Space, 2014

*Merrill F. Unger, Zechariah: Prophet of God's Glory, Zondervan, 2014

A Snapshot of Malachi

Author

Malachi

Date of Writing

@420 B.C. (during the time when Nehemiah was back in Suza. (432-420 B.C.)

Recipients

The Jews who had returned from the Babylonian exile.

Theme

A right relationship with God is moral and not ceremonial.

Purpose

To revive the spiritual lives of the remnant.

Outline

1. Issues of contention 1:1-3:15

   1) Forgotten identity. I :2-5

   2) Dishonorable worship.**1:6-2:9**

   3) Unholy marriages. 2:10-16

   4) Distortion of the truth. 2: 17-3:6

5) Disobedience in tithing. 3:7-12

6) Disloyal secularism. 3:13-15

2. Response of the righteous 3:16a

3. Final prophecies and admonition 3:16b-4:6

Characteristics and Points of Interest

1. Under the Persian yoke the Jews were in poor shape: spiritually disconsolate, insensitive to God's love, slack in worship, ritualistic, unaware of their condition, secular in viewpoint, and behind all this is bitterness a belief that God has not brought the prophetic promises to fulfillment.

2. Each section is set apart by Malachi's unique question and answer format. God states a fault; they ask an incredulous question; God answers by clarifying the problem and stating the consequences.

3. Malachi is the last Old Testament prophet. Only more than 400 years later does God send John in fulfillment of the last prophecy in Malachi. (Whether John the Baptist fully fulfills the prophecy of 4:5-6 is debatable.) cf. Matthew 17: 12-13

Major Applications

1. Man is often unaware of his true spiritual condition.

2. The danger of insensitivity to God's love.

3. God will only accept worship given in spirit and truth.

4. Instruction is given to turn people back from iniquity.

5. God hates divorce. Marriage is a covenant before God.

6. God will purify His children by chastening.

7. Proper response to God's Word will not be forgotten by God.

8. God will bring justice for the righteous.

Recommended Resources

Charles L. Feinberg, The Minor Prophets, Moody, 1976

Walter Kaiser, Malachi: God's Unchanging Love, Baker, 1984

John L. Mackay, Haggai, Zechariah, and Malachi: God's Restored People, Christian Focus, 2010

Thomas E. McComiskey, The Minor Prophets: A Commentary on Zephaniah, Haggai,

 Zechariah, and Malachi, Baker, 2018

*Allen P. Ross, Malachi: Then & Now: An Expository Commentary, Lexham Press, 2016

Peter Verhoef, The Books of Haggai and Malachi, [NICOT] Eerdmans, 198

www.ingramcontent.com/pod-product-compliance
Lightning Source LLC
Chambersburg PA
CBHW021622120626
46545CB00001B/352